SACRAMENTO PUBLIC LIBRARY

3 3029 04903 2832

Climb

ELK GROVE LIBRARY
8962 ELK GROVE BOULEVARD
ELK GROVE, CA 95624

Advance praise from the (
Climb On! Skills for Mc 7-03

"Just great! Guess all of our hard-won secrets are out. Guess all my records are going to be taken away now. Great, just freakin' great!"

—Steve Schneider

"Inspiring and joyful! Makes you want to travel light, go fast, and be a better player on the team."

—Tom Frost

"This book is not just for a few, highly skilled climbers who have elevated the sport to a high art. This is for those of us who want to get down without bivvying, beat a thunderstorm, or get in a raft of pitches in the few pathetic hours we have available. It is a trove of practical information—detailed yet accessible, sprightly and humorous. Hans Florine is a very great force in our sport. Creative and responsible, he has contributed in more ways than most climbers could know, from setting rad Yosemite and High Sierra records to volunteering for years as the director of the American Sport Climbing Federation. Hans has always been a superior competitor because as hard as he tries to do his best, and to best the next climber, he truly wishes others well. He is the first to congratulate and appreciate a peer who breaks one of his records (then to grab a rope and try again). This book is a way of wishing all of us well."

—Alison Osius, Senior Editor,
Climbing magazine, author, and
former national champion in sport climbing

D0197342

How to Climb Series

Climb On!

Skills for More Efficient Climbing

by Hans Florine and Bill Wright

FALCON®

GUILFORD, CONNECTICUT
An imprint of The Globe Pequot Press

Copyright © 2002 by The Globe Pequot Press

All rights reserved. No part of this book may be reproduced or transmitted in any form by any means, electronic or mechanical, including photocopying and recording, or by any information storage and retrieval system, except as may be expressly permitted by the 1976 Copyright Act or by the publisher. Requests for permission should be made in writing to The Globe Pequot Press, P.O. Box 480, Guilford, Connecticut 06437.

Falcon and FalconGuide are registered trademarks of The Globe Pequot Press.

Cover design: Libby Kingsbury
Cover photo: Gregg Epperson/Index Stock
Text design: Lisa Reneson
Illustrations: Greg Opland
Climbing topo on pages 112–113 courtesy and permission of SuperTopo

Library of Congress Cataloging-in-Publication Data
Florine, Hans.
   Climb on!: skills for more efficient climbing/by Hans Florine and Bill Wright.—1st ed.
      p.cm. — (How to climb series)
   Includes bibliographical references.
   ISBN 0-7627-1168-X
   1. Rock climbing. I. Wright, Bill, 1962– II. Title. III. Series.
GV200.2 .F58 2002
796.52'23—dc21   2001053197

Manufactured in the United States of America
First edition/First printing

Contents

HANS FLORINE

Hans Florine lives in California with wife Jacqueline and daughter
Marianna. Hans was a U.S. National Champion in Difficulty and Speed
Climbing, a World Champion in Speed Climbing, and a three-time gold
medalist in Speed Climbing at the X-Games. He holds numerous speed
records in outdoor climbing, from sport routes to alpine. Hans com-
petes in just about anything and was an All-American in the Pole Vault.
He received a BS in Economics from California Polytechnic State
University. For four years Hans was the executive director of the American
Sport Climbers Federation, the governing body for competitive climbing
in the United States. He describes himself as an Objectivist in the tradition of the writer Ayn Rand. He is a professional climber, writer, photographer, and outdoor guide who teaches and promotes the sport of
climbing.

BILL WRIGHT

Bill Wright is a software engineer who lives in Superior, Colorado, with
his wife Sheri and two sons, Daniel Layton and Derek Logan. Bill spent
nine years working in the Bay Area and climbing most of the structures in
Yosemite. In order to balance his passions for climbing and family life,
Bill has turned more and more toward speed climbing. Bill has climbed
on three different continents and enjoys alpine climbing, big walls, and
cragging.

Preface

HANS FLORINE

I'm indebted to Steve Schneider, who taught me many of the big wall skills I've included in this book. (I'm sure he's torn up inside that he didn't beat me to writing one of his own.) Back in 1990 Steve agreed to climb the Nose on Yosemite's El Capitan with me based purely on my brash claim that I was the "world's fastest human on the vertical." After Steve endured me bringing my parents (and their photographer) to the base of El Cap and then me whipping 25 feet on the second pitch, I knew he must have liked me—anyone else would have called it quits right there and rapped off. (Of course, Steve didn't mind the beer and sandwiches my mom and dad had waiting for us in the parking lot—heck, maybe that's what won him over, not my climbing.)

I've been lucky to climb with many great partners in my life. I tend to keep trying new ones—not because the people I've climbed with aren't great, but because I like the different experience each person brings to climbing. I've learned a little from everyone, whether they climb 5.7 or 5.14, A0 or A5. Rather than listing all the partners I've shared a rope with and possibly forgetting someone, I'll just say thanks to all of you for keeping me safe—and keeping me from forced bivies.

As for Bill Wright, he basically threatened me by saying that if I didn't write a book on speed climbing, he would do it without me. Bill must have known that the competitive blood was boiling within me; he knew just the right thing to say to make me sign on the dotted line. You can all thank Bill for the fact that this book is coming out two to ten years earlier than would otherwise have been the case.

I have to thank my wife Jacqueline who contends she's a "total bumbly." She is not of course, with seven El Cap ascents under her belt to date, three while pregnant with our daughter Marianna, and numerous other Yosemite big wall ascents. She's been a great person to bounce ideas off of—she claims that she represents the bumblies and that if she can understand what Bill and I are writing about, then anyone can.

One of the most rewarding experiences for me is when someone tells me I've inspired them. Included in this book are not just the dry facts of "how to climb fast" but also real-life stories contributed by some of my climbing partners with the express purpose of inspiring you to *use* this book's dry facts when doing your own climbs. Many of my partners hold 9-to-5 jobs yet still manage to bust out incredibly huge Sierra and Yosemite weekend adventures—adventures that often make my full-time climbing exploits seem average. These people have inspired me more than they know. I hope their stories inspire you as well.

Hans Florine

BILL WRIGHT

The struggle itself toward the heights is enough to fill man's heart. One must imagine Sisyphus happy.

–Albert Camus, *The Myth of Sisyphus*

I love climbing—climbing up anything at all. From hiking up a trail to pedaling up steep pavement, from skinning up a snow slope to jamming up a crack, I love to climb. There is something in the struggle against gravity that elates me. I used to think that climbing was a passing fancy and that once I'd climbed El Cap, I'd move on to other adventures. I know now that isn't true. I'm a lifer.

I decided to write this book for many reasons, but the most overwhelming reason was because *I* wanted to have such a book. Despite the fact that speed climbing has a rich history and has been part of our sport for many years, up until now no book has been available on the subject. I finally figured out that if I wanted such a book, I'd have to write it myself—along with Hans, of course.

This brings me to another reason I wanted to take on this project—the opportunity to work with Hans Florine, the "master of speed climbing." Getting to know Hans and sharing a rope with him has been a thrill, like playing baseball with Babe Ruth.

I am frequently frustrated by the media's superficial coverage of awesome climbing feats. There seems to be an incredible disregard for the obvious question "How did they go that fast?" Certainly other climbers have wondered the same thing. This book is my attempt to answer that question for myself and anybody else who has ever found themselves wondering the same thing.

You might be asking yourself "Who is Bill Wright and why should I read what he's written?" Well, I'm nobody really—but in a sense I'm everybody. At the very least I'm probably a typical weekend climber. But, you ask, "If you're so typical, what do you have to say that might be of interest to me?" I act here mainly as an interviewer, researcher, and writer. I was as curious about the techniques of the super speed climbers as perhaps you are now. While I do practice speed climbing, I do it at a modest level—just like I climb at a modest level. Hence, I'm proof that the techniques in this book aren't just for the superstars but will prove useful for every weekender in search of more climbing.

While many climbers have influenced me, there is one climber who prompted me to fundamentally reexamine my own climbing—Jim Herson. For years I had been interested in speed climbing, but mostly in an armchair manner. However, in June 1999 my partner, Tom Karpeichik, and I were just starting up the Salathé Wall on El Capitan in Yosemite National Park. We were climbing the first ten pitches, known as The Free Blast, so that we could fix ropes down from Heart Ledges. We then planned on spending the next three and a half days climbing and hauling our way to the top. This is the standard approach to climbing the Salathé. Our speed was probably about average.

As is often the case, it was a zoo at the start of the route that morning. No less than four parties were jockeying for position on the route. We were there first and moving steadily up the route, but there was another team right on our heels. As I finished leading the fourth pitch, a 5.10b crack, Tom told me that we were going to let another party pass us. I looked down expecting to see the white helmets of the team that had been behind us all morning; but no, the passers were a different party altogether. I was amazed. How could these guys have already passed the White Helmets and now be poised to pass us? They hadn't even hiked to the base of the route by the time I jugged the third pitch, and now they were going by us. I watched as a lean Frank Shorter look-alike practically ran up the 5.10 pitch like some sort of climbing machine, only placing a couple pieces of protection. (Frank Shorter was the last American to win a gold medal in the Olympic marathon in 1972.) The climber said hello as he clipped a draw into the anchor and, without pausing, moved on up the next pitch! This was my introduction to Jim Herson.

I noticed Herson's climbing rack was tiny—about one-third the size of our rack. He was climbing the Salathé (notorious for wide pitches) with nothing bigger than his single #3 Camalot. We learned from his partner,

Peter Coward, that Jim was trying to redpoint the entire Salathé Wall. (At the time only four people had redpointed every pitch on the Salathé: Alex and Thomas Huber, Yuji Hirayama, and Tommy Caldwell.) Clearly Jim was a world-class climber, but that wasn't the most striking aspect of his ascent. What amazed me was that these two were climbing the Salathé in a day and a half. They were climbing it like it was a local crag route. They were just going up to see if they could climb it clean, like I had done with single-pitch routes near my home. They climbed with a tiny rack and a small pack, and moved lightning fast. It was a different sport than what Tom and I were practicing; we were inching up the rock in painstaking fashion. To compare our ascent to Herson and Coward's is to compare a marathoner with a miler. They were free climbing and moving fast; we were mired in such mundane tasks as hauling bags. It was a big adventure for us, one that we had planned for an entire year; but to Jim it was just the route he'd decided to climb when he woke up that day.

Later that season Jim climbed the Salathé again with Chandlee Harrell. This time he wasn't going for the redpoint and hence was able to climb considerably faster. They did the entire 35-pitch route in six and a half hours! Once again, I was amazed. I wanted to enter this world and I began researching in earnest. This led to a correspondence and eventually a friendship with Hans, and even Jim Herson.

Speed climbing feats have been reported in a number of books and magazines but never meticulously recorded. I haven't changed that here, but merely have made an attempt to compile some of its rich history. I've tried to focus on the climbs that have changed attitudes. I have left much out due to limitations of space. Additional sources for speed climbing history can be found in the *2000 American Alpine Club Journal*, Climbing #153 and #203. I've also left out any history of formal speed competition climbing at this time. I do have visions of writing a more complete history someday, so if you have any information about speed climbing in other areas, please e-mail me at bill@wwwright.com.

Because I might never write another book, I want to acknowledge and thank the great partners I've had throughout the years. I needed partners that were more at my level but had the enthusiasm for the same goals. (Jim Herson and I would no sooner rope up together than Michael Jordan would play pick-up ball at the local playground.) In that respect I feel I am probably the luckiest climber in the world. My circle of climbing partners is the best anywhere. I'll risk offending some partners and list names. I'll also apologize ahead of time for anyone left out. Special mention has to go to three partners: Lou "The Loobster" Lorber, George "Trashman" Bell, and Tom "Hardly Manson" Karpeichik. They have an insatiable desire for climbing in all its forms. There are no finer climbers or individuals anywhere. They are the rawest definition of a climbing *partner*. These three will, and have, given me the shirt off their backs. There is no "mine" with them. Everything is *ours*. They never complain, never tire, and never turn down an adventure.

There are many more partners—too many to completely list. I've learned from them all and enjoyed climbing with them. Such lifelong friendships may be climbing's greatest reward. I thank Bruce "Dr. Offwidth" Bailey, Eric "Tinky Winky" Winkelman, John "Homie" Prater, Mark "White Rim" Oveson, John "Berries" Black, Greg "Opie" Opland, Steve "Bowling Ball" Mathias, and the rest of the Satan's Minions Scrambling Club for climbing with me.

Of course, I must thank Hans Florine for agreeing to work with me on this book and for his boundless generosity in sharing his home, his knowledge, and his spirit. Heck, I even got to climb with him!

Finally, my greatest joy: my family. My wife, Sheri, a serious athlete herself, is the love of my life. She makes it possible for me to pursue climbing. She understands that life is a balancing act and she keeps me from toppling over. She has also given me two great little boys: Daniel and Derek. I can't wait for these two to guide me up Everest—in record time, no less!

Bill Wright

WARNING:
CLIMBING IS A SPORT WHERE YOU MAY BE SERIOUSLY INJURED OR DIE. READ THIS BEFORE YOU USE THIS BOOK.

This guidebook is a compilation of unverified information gathered from many different climbers. The author cannot assure the accuracy of any of the information in this book, including the topos and route descriptions, the difficulty ratings, and the protection ratings. These may be incorrect or misleading and it is impossible for any one author to climb all the routes to confirm the information about each route. Also, ratings of climbing difficulty and danger are always subjective and depend on the physical characteristics (for example, height), experience, technical ability, confidence, and physical fitness of the climber who supplied the rating. Additionally, climbers who achieve first ascents sometimes underrate the difficulty or danger of the climbing route out of fear of being ridiculed if a climb is later down-rated by subsequent ascents. Therefore, be warned that you must exercise your own judgment on where a climbing route goes, its difficulty, and your ability to safely protect yourself from the risks of rock climbing. Examples of some of these risks are: falling due to technical difficulty or due to natural hazards such as holds breaking, falling rock, climbing equipment dropped by other climbers, hazards of weather and lightning, your own equipment failure, and failure or absence of fixed protection.

You should not depend on any information gleaned from this book for your personal safety; your safety depends on your own good judgment, based on experience and a realistic assessment of your climbing ability. If you have any doubt as to your ability to safely climb a route described in this book, do not attempt it.

The following are some ways to make your use of this book safer:

1. Consultation: You should consult with other climbers about the difficulty and danger of a particular climb prior to attempting it. Most local climbers are glad to give advice on routes in their area and we suggest that you contact locals to confirm ratings and safety of particular routes and to obtain first-hand information about a route chosen from this book.

2. Instruction: Most climbing areas have local climbing instructors and guides available. We recommend that you engage an instructor or guide to learn safety techniques and to become familiar with the routes and hazards of the areas described in this book. Even after you are proficient in climbing safely, occasional use of a guide is a safe way to raise your climbing standard and learn advanced techniques.

3. Fixed Protection: Many of the routes in this book use bolts and pitons which are permanently placed in the rock. Because of variances in the manner of placement, weathering, metal fatigue, the quality of the metal used, and many other factors, these fixed protection pieces should always be considered suspect and should always be backed up by equipment that you place yourself. Never depend for your safety on a single piece of fixed protection because you never can tell whether it will hold weight, and in some cases, fixed protection may have been removed or is now absent.

Be aware of the following specific potential hazards that could arise in using this book:

1. Misdescriptions of Routes: If you climb a route and you have a doubt as to where the route may go, you should not go on unless you are sure that you can go that way safely. Route descriptions and topos in this book may be inaccurate or misleading.

2. Incorrect Difficulty Rating: A route may, in fact, be more difficult than the rating indicates. Do not be lulled into a false sense of security by the difficulty rating.

3. Incorrect Protection Rating: If you climb a route and you are unable to arrange adequate protection from the risk of falling through the use of fixed pitons or bolts and by placing your own protection devices, do not assume that there is adequate protection available higher just because the route protection rating indicates the route is not an "X" or an "R" rating. Every route is potentially an "X" (a fall may be deadly), due to the inherent hazards of climbing—including, for example, failure or absence of fixed protection, your own equipment's failure, or improper use of climbing equipment.

THERE ARE NO WARRANTIES, WHETHER EXPRESS OR IMPLIED, THAT THIS GUIDEBOOK IS ACCURATE OR THAT THE INFORMATION CONTAINED IN IT IS RELIABLE. THERE ARE NO WARRANTIES OF FITNESS FOR A PARTICULAR PURPOSE OR THAT THIS GUIDE IS MERCHANTABLE. YOUR USE OF THIS BOOK INDICATES YOUR ASSUMPTION OF THE RISK THAT IT MAY CONTAIN ERRORS AND IS AN ACKNOWLEDGMENT OF YOUR OWN SOLE RESPONSIBILITY FOR YOUR CLIMBING SAFETY.

CHAPTER 1

SPEED CLIMBING: WHAT IS IT AND WHY DO IT?

Dream barriers look very high until someone climbs them. Then they are not barriers anymore.

—Lasse Viren, one of the greatest distance runners of all time

What is speed climbing? To some it's what they see on TV—the X-Games, where people climb 12 seconds on a 50-foot plastic wall. To others it's plugging away up a 3,000-foot El Cap route in a day. Speed climbing is many different things to many different people, but at its most basic level, speed climbing is a philosophy about moving quickly and efficiently up difficult terrain. It doesn't have to be an all-out race for the world record. Maybe you just want to do a big route in a day. Or, it could be just about setting a personal record on a route—much as you might do while running your favorite trail. This book is not about how to burn the rubber off the bottom of your climbing shoes—it's about getting in more climbing on your climbing days. We wrote this book because we believe that the only thing better than climbing is *more* climbing!

All the tips in this book aren't for everyone to practice. Carefully consider those that you can utilize and discard the others. Keep in mind that the more tips you use, the more climbing you'll do on your weekends—and the bigger your smile will be while you daydream at the office Monday morning. The constant desire to improve and learn the more efficient/faster way to do a task can really change what you are able to do in a day—or in an evening after work.

Speed climbing is fun. Speed climbing lets you climb more, but it clearly isn't everything. It holds no interest for some climbers, though most climbers would benefit from at least knowing the techniques and applying them, however sparingly, to their own climbing. We don't speed climb all the time. In fact, for me (B.W.) at least, it is the exception rather than the rule. Legendary French climber, Gaston Rébuffat, wrote in

The Snowball Effect of Big Wall Planning

Most people haul tons of gear up an El Cap route not because they want to savor the experience of carrying all this stuff, but because they can't climb the route in one day. Let's take a look at what happens when you can't climb the route in a single day. You have to take bivy gear, right? Maybe a porta-ledge. Certainly more food and water. Without this extra weight maybe you could do the route in, say, a day and a half; but now it will take you two and a half days because you're going slower hauling all this additional gear and setting up and tearing down the bivouac. So now you need gear for two and a half days, which involves more water and food, slowing you down further. It's the proverbial "snowball effect" of big wall climbing.

the introduction to his classic book *Starlight and Storm,* ". . . some mountaineers are proud of having done all their climbs without bivouac. How much they have missed!" And despite the fact that Hans sports a license plate that reads "NoBivys," we've both taken time to smell the Alpine roses, via a bivouac.

Speed climbing doesn't mean that you race up the rock so fast that you can't enjoy the climbing or admire the views or revel in the solitude of your position. You could liken it to going on a trail run versus a backpacking trip. On the trail run you are moving much less encumbered and flowing easily over the terrain. You cover the same distance in a long run as on a two-day backpacking trip. Is one better than the other? Not really. It certainly depends on the person. Each experience has its rewards.

Even an average team planning to climb the Nose in three days can benefit from speed climbing techniques. The Nose has good bivy ledges distributed along the route. If you are fast enough to reach these ledges each day, then you won't have to haul up a porta-ledge or an uncomfortable hammock. This ability to climb fast and get to the bivy ledges means you haul less weight and waste less time setting up and tearing down the bivy. Hence, even though the ascent is not done in a single push, the techniques discussed in this book can increase your enjoyment of the climbing by decreasing the drudgery of hauling unnecessary weight.

Chandlee Harrel in front of Mt. Goode on just another weekend outing—if you speed climb. (Greg Murphy)

Success Versus Failure on the Direct North Buttress
by Bill Wright

While getting ready to attempt the Direct North Buttress (DNB) of Middle Cathedral Rock in Yosemite in mid-November, my partner Jim Merritt and I got to talking about the "multiplication of supplies." It started by simply reading the label on our energy bars, which said to "eat one every hour with a quart of water while exercising." "Well," we thought, "we're definitely exercising."

The DNB is a serious, devious route that's 20 pitches. Jim and I were in over our heads a bit—being somewhat slow climbers—so we decided on a two-day ascent, which meant hauling bivy gear up the route. We would be working about ten hours a day for two days. If we each ate one energy bar per hour with the recommended one quart of water, we calculated the amount of water we would have to haul would equal 40 quarts (2 people x 10 hours x 2 days x 1 quart of water). Because there is two pints in a quart and "a pint's a pound the world around," we would have to carry 80 pounds of water alone.

Of course, this is way too much water for a north-facing wall in mid-November, but that's not my point. My point is that if we had hauled 80 pounds of water, it probably would have taken us twice as long to climb the wall—but then we'd have needed to haul twice as many energy bars and twice as much water! You can see where this is leading. Pretty soon we'd be so weighed down that we wouldn't be able to get off the ground.

We could have used siege tactics to climb the DNB and solved our lack-of-speed problem. The first big walls were climbed using siege tactics for exactly this reason. El Cap was first climbed this way, as were other big walls in Yosemite. But we didn't want to climb the route that way, not necessarily because of some ethical dilemma—heck, we were just a couple of weekend warriors who weren't trying to prove anything to anybody—but because we didn't have the time or resources for such a prolonged battle.

In the end, we ended up retreating off the DNB. We just weren't fast enough to make the climb and leave ourselves a reasonable safety margin. We didn't really need to be better technical climbers, though of course that would have helped. We just needed to be faster, more efficient climbers. Our objective wasn't to set a personal record on the route but to do the climb in a more enjoyable manner and succeed in topping out on the route.

Reasons to Speed Climb

The reasons for climbing fast are as numerous as the reasons to climb at all. In alpine climbing, speed is safety. The less time you spend exposed to objective dangers such as avalanches and rockfall, the safer you are. Maybe you just want to move more efficiently with the least amount of down time. When you call up your partner to make a plan for the weekend, you don't ask, "Want to go belaying tomorrow?" or, "Want to haul a big bag up El Cap tomorrow?" No, you want to go climbing! The rest of that crap is just an evil necessity, not a joy to be prolonged.

Climbing fast not only cuts down on the extraneous chores, but it provides for more comfortable nights. When asked why he climbs so fast, the great French speed climber, Jean-Marc Boivin, said, "The fact is that at night I'd rather sleep with Françoise than in a cold bivouac in an ice hole!" Touché.

What about sport climbers doing one- or two-pitch routes without the prospect of a cold bivy? Well, simply put, going faster will make you a better climber. Climbing hard routes at the limit of your ability is frequently a race against muscular failure; and the faster you are, the better chance you have to win that race. Getting to the top before you pump out equals success on a sport route.

By far the best reason to speed climb is because it's fun. Remember, the only thing better than climbing is *more* climbing. Climbing fast enables you to climb more pitches, complete more routes, and go more places. Whether that means moving quickly up a route without extraneous distractions or blasting up a route at your absolute limit, speed climbing is fun. As Miles Smart, holder of numerous Yosemite speed records, says, "Stripped down and going light is when [climbing] really becomes fun."

"In Defense of Speed Records . . ."

Some will say that climbing a route to set a speed record is silly and that time is better spent pushing the level of difficulty or forging a new route.

Throwing Tradition to the Wind on the Nose
by Hans Florine

In 1987 I tried to climb the Nose with my buddy Mike Lopez. We got off route on the second pitch and nearly fell to our death when a pin came out and left the two of us and the haul bag dangling on *one* small nut. It took us most of the day just to get to Sickle Ledge, just four pitches off the ground. We ate some food there and decided that we should bail, so we rappelled the four rope-lengths back to the ground. We made it to the valley floor before dark—barely.

The next year we came back, "weekend warrior bumblies" that we were. We arrived in the meadow Saturday at 6 P.M. on the three-day 4th of July weekend. We were a bit ignorant about "how it's supposed to be done." Despite the fact that it was late in the day, we thought, "What the heck, lets jump on it!" This was at 7 P.M. We climbed until we couldn't climb any longer, under a full moon and all. We stopped on Sickle Ledge for a two-hour nap but made it to Dolt Tower by Sunday at noon.

We slept on El Cap Tower in the afternoon for a few hours, continued to climb through the next night, and finally were so whipped we stopped on the ledge at Camp V for six hours of sleep. We topped out on Monday at 1 P.M. It was a 42-hour ascent—onsight (kind of). We drank caffeine, drove back home, and made it to classes on Tuesday!

We did this route fast out of necessity, I suppose, but we also did it by saying, "To hell with how it's supposed to be done! We've got two days—let's get on it!" The next time I did the Nose was two years later with Steve Schneider. We made the climb in eight hours. Three years after that I made it to Sickle Ledge with Peter Croft in 26 minutes—the same distance that took me nearly a whole day my first try seven years prior!

For some climbers this is undoubtedly true. But just like there are Olympic divers who push the difficulty of their acrobatics each year, there are also Olympic swimmers who are driven to continually set new world speed records. For some of us, blasting up a route quickly, especially onsight, can be just as adventurous as putting up a new route or climbing a route at the limit of our ability. In fact, it can often be much more of an adventure. A new aid route entails a lot more belaying, hauling, and sleeping on porta-ledges than it does actual climbing. Speed climbing, on the other hand, maximizes the actual time spent climbing.

Some people are put off by the overtly competitive atmosphere of the Yosemite Valley speed climbers. While it's true this atmosphere isn't for everyone, it's also true that many are motivated by competition. In every other sport, competition has brought out the best in the participants. In fact, almost every significant climber's résumé will include at least some mention of a fast time on a particular route. Even sport climbers will mention how fast they redpointed a certain route. Climbing a route fast doesn't require joining some unsanctioned speed competition, it just requires that you enjoy moving faster over the rock.

My First Speed Climb
by Bill Wright, July 1999

After dinner Hans agreed to climb the next day and asks me, "What about the East Buttress of Lower Cathedral Rock?" I say, "That would be fine. I've done it before, but climbing anything with you would be great." He says, "The East Buttress of *Lower* Cathedral Rock." He obviously thought I was thinking about the classic and very popular East Buttress of *Middle* Cathedral Rock.

I had climbed this 12-pitch, 5.10c route with the Loobster in 1996. I had led every pitch and it had taken us most of the day. We were snowed on during the last couple of pitches on that ascent. Hans had done the route once before also (with Roxanne Brock), and he was off route for the first two pitches, off route in the middle, and off route at the top. Hence, he was anxious to climb the entire route. I would be his guide! Hans felt his variations were more like 5.11c.

On the drive to the route, Hans briefed me on how he likes to do things. He gives a one-minute warning when he is approaching the end of a pitch so that the second climber can get ready to go as soon as possible. Hans doesn't simul-climb unless he is 100 percent sure that the other person will not fall. Hans doesn't usually carry stoppers and for this route he brought only four stoppers and no nut tool. I remembered placing stoppers galore on the crux pitch and I am particularly fond of this type of protection, but I deferred to the master. Heck, he'd lead the crux pitch anyway.

We parked below Lower Cathedral Rock and threw on the packs. I immediately led us up a talus slope too far to the right. Hans got us back on track and I led us to the start of the intimidating 5.8 chimney that marks the start of the route. It took us only 16 minutes to get to the base of the route, but then we'd lounged around taking time to gear up. We'd later regret this when deciding to go for a car-to-car time.

We both wore shorts and kneepads for the chimney. I pulled on my tape gloves, but Hans said he rarely ever tapes up. I wore a T-shirt, and my Camelbak was our only water. Hans stripped off this shirt to reveal a chiseled physique. I was surprised he'd climb without a shirt in such a chimney and didn't follow suit. Of course, I had no chiseled body to reveal—only a belly pouring over the top of my harness.

Hans is very strict about when to start and stop the watch for speed ascents. (This is detailed on his Web site www. speedclimb.com.) We both wore watches and started them just as Hans took off on the first pitch. Hans scooted up the 160-foot chimney in 11 minutes and soon I was following. I pulled onto the ledge huffing and puffing ten minutes later. Hans led the next 160-foot pitch also, which has a short 5.10a section, but Hans barely paused. Following this section, I was trying to hurry, and I made a mistake and almost fell off, but I corrected and continued up.

Now it was my turn to lead. Hans handed me the Spartan rack, which included just one #4, #3, #2, and #1 Camalots. The rest were all smaller cams, mostly TCUs, and of course, the four stoppers. We had only three long slings and five or six quick draws. I guess I was getting ready to learn one trick of speed climbing: carry a small rack. You are going light, and you don't have much gear to stop and place. I was definitely into the speed-climbing mode and didn't want to let Hans down. Though I knew our pace was going to drop, I was determined not to let it drop too far.

I raced up the Fissure Beck pitch (5.9) and wrestled with the leaning 5.9 squeeze. I ran things out much farther than I normally would—about 20 feet between placements. I finished the pitch at the hanging tree belay just after Hans called the halfway mark, so I continued up the next pitch, which is 5.8. I stretched out all the rope and placed most of the rack before I got to the tiny ledge. I set up a belay with one stopper, and a #2 and #4 Camalot. I was feeling good having led two pitches so quickly, and Hans followed in a flash.

I offered to pull one of the pieces out of the belay, but he declined and fired up the tricky, stemming/finger crack crux pitch. Hans did some huge stems on this pitch that I knew I couldn't duplicate. Hans is "6 foot 1 in the morning," as he says, and I'm only 5 foot 11. Hans is also very flexible and no one would mistake me for a gymnast. I fell off leading this pitch before and warned Hans that I might come off. He reassured me that if I wanted to take some more time and get it free, that was fine with him.

Hans ran out most of the rope and it was my turn. I negotiated the lower section pretty quickly and was faced with the crux. Because I couldn't do the stem, I had to climb the corner directly and this involved dicey body wedging and desperate reaches to shallow finger jams. Breathing like a steam engine, I barely scraped through without coming off and let out a victory yell. I motored up to Hans and he took the next 5.7 pitch as I was still breathing hard.

I followed and showed Hans the proper way to turn the roof on the next pitch. Hans had previously gone directly up to the roof thinking that turning it on the right looked intimidating. I cruised up the right side at 5.9 and belayed at a tree. Hans followed and commented how nice it was to be on route. I took off on the next 5.6 pitch and Hans told me to just keep going if I felt good. He'd simul-climb behind me. I put the next 5.9 pitch together with the long 5.6 pitch and half of the next 5.7 pitch up to a ledge before I belayed. I had gone for two and a half pitches and was pretty much out of gear. I checked the watch and it indicated we had been climbing for two hours and 43 minutes.

I said to Hans as he took over the lead, "If we hurry, we can break three hours." His reply was, "We'll break three hours and we won't have to hurry." When the rope came tight, I started up. The upper half of this climb is a bit junky and moss-covered, with some loose rock and runouts interspersed with some good climbing. I flew up the last section to Hans and we stopped the watches: 2 hours and 58 minutes. Not bad for 12 pitches. Hans commented that we could possibly do the route in under 4 hours car-to-car, and the race was on.

So much for taking in the great views from the summit. This is certainly a drawback of speed climbing. John Orenschall once said "Climbing would be a great, truly wonderful thing if it weren't for all that damn climbing." Well, speed climbing could be a great, truly wonderful thing if it weren't for all that damn rushing around.

We scrambled down the Gunsight, downclimbing all the rappels, back to our packs. We downed more liquids and packed up. It was going to be tight, very tight. After getting down the steepest sections and off the talus, we were running through the woods. It was fun pursuing such a ridiculous goal with Hans. We are very much alike in that regard. We jumped over logs and dodged trees until we hit the road. A quick dash to Hans's truck and I stopped the watch: 3 hours and 58 minutes. No problem!

Basically, we're firm believers in the power of competition to drive humans to better their achievements. Blatant competition is healthy! The Brits call it burning off your mates; we call it building on your mates' achievements. It inspires us to do bigger, better, faster feats, and in turn, we hopefully inspire others to get off the sofa and improve on their own achievements.

Setting speed climbing records is not for everyone. Many people relish the time spent on a wall and, instead of wanting to go faster, seem to stretch things out so that they can prolong their time in the vertical world. El Cap has been climbed in as little as 1 hour and 56 minutes, and as long as 39 days! Some people like to just slow down and smell the copperheads. Others, as Maverick says in the movie *Top Gun*, just "feel the need—the need for speed!"

Consider a fellow named Jason Wening. Wening isn't a climber; he's a disabled swimmer. But he understands the need for speed—he holds six world records in disabled swimming. When asked why he pushes himself so hard, he responded, "For the simple pleasure of forcing the body and mind I was given to the absolute edge of my capabilities. I'm fascinated by trying to go even faster. And when I do, I get for just a moment a vision of the limitless potential of the human race."

Best view in the valley—looking down the Nose from the last pitch. (Hans Florine)

Be Careful Out There (A Disclaimer)

Rock climbing is a dangerous sport, and speed climbing carries with it certain risks. If you don't understand this, then you probably shouldn't be reading this book. Yes, the dangers can be mitigated and we've both climbed thousands of routes without getting killed. (Bill did break his back in a rappelling accident, although he recovered quickly and three months later broke the record for climbing the "Top Ten" Flatiron routes with Tom Karpeichik.) The point is that you can get away with taking risks time after time, but don't get lulled into a false sense of security. Speed does NOT equate to unsafe, certainly not for Hans and Bill.

As Bill's experience emphasizes, accidents do happen, so don't let your guard down. In a sport such as tennis, if you fail, the worst that can happen is you lose the point. In climbing, however, a bad mistake can kill you. There's another important distinction between tennis and climbing.

In tennis you have a split second to make a decision and execute a shot, and it is difficult to be "on" every time under these rapid-fire circumstances. In climbing, however, you have plenty of time to make the right decision. There is no time limit in most cases. Even though this book is about climbing faster, these speed techniques must be tempered with good common sense. Take enough time to make sure you and your partner are safe. Be certain that you are doing everything right, and then re-check everything again. If things look good, continue from there.

That may seem like a contradiction. If the advantage climbing has over tennis is that in climbing you have unlimited time to make decisions, how does that reconcile with speed climbing? You'll find as you read through the book we don't advocate rushing decisions; we have you eliminate unnecessary actions and methods and make more efficient movements. In some cases, climbing fast is safer than climbing slow. Certainly with a bad storm approaching, it is advantageous to move fast so that you can get off the climb, either up or down, and seek shelter.

Having said that, we want you to remember that some of the techniques specified in this book can be dangerous if you don't use good judgment when implementing them. Decide which techniques will work for you, take what you can from this book, and use it to get in tons of climbing—but be careful!

CHAPTER 2
MULTIPITCH CLIMBS

Insecurities about safety certainly slow people down.
—Mark Melvin, Bay Area speed climber.

This chapter doesn't attempt to describe everything involved in climbing multipitch routes. John Long and Craig Luebben's book *Advanced Rock Climbing* is a good reference for climbing systems, belaying, descending, equipment, etc. We are going to deal with techniques that are specific to efficient climbing. You will learn a variety of ways to increase your speed. In Long and Luebben's book, there is a line about simul-climbing (a technique discussed in our Chapter 4) that reads ". . . whatever situation might force you into simul-climbing, vaya con Dios." Go with God! Well, that's not our sentiment. We will share "fringe" techniques that allow you to move fast.

Getting Started
Every type of climbing is potentially dangerous, and speed climbing isn't any different; but if you are afraid, you won't be able to move as fast as you can. You should know your safety system so well that you can make last minute changes without hesitation. At belays you want to stay clipped into two independent and secure links, but these two links might not be what you're used to.

When climbing fast on multipitch routes, the typical sequence of events should go something like this. The lead climber blasts up the pitch with reckless abandon. That's what you expected right? Going fast by being reckless? I (H.F.) am just making sure you're paying attention. No, the leader moves efficiently and safely up the pitch and yells down a one-minute (or two-minute) warning as she gets close to the next anchor. This allows the belayer to get ready to move by breaking down unnecessary anchor points, putting on his backpack, lacing up his shoes—getting

Chandlee Harrel having fun on the long push on Tis-sa-ack. (Greg Murphy)

ready to rock. The instant the leader says "Off belay" and then "Rope fixed" or "On belay," the follower can start up.

To this point I'm assuming there is a fixed anchor station at the end of the pitch, or at least a clear belay location. In the event that there is no clear belay, the second might yell up "30 feet!" so the leader knows she's approaching the end of the line. This gives the leader some notice to decide where to set up a belay. Occasionally you will not find a solid belay spot before running out of rope. If this situation is likely to occur, you should discuss a plan of action with your partner before leaving the ground. The likely outcome may be to simul-climb until you reach a suitable belay.

It should be standard procedure for the belayer to call out "Halfway!" when half of the rope has been consumed by the leader. This gives the leader some idea of her climbing rate and her location on the pitch. She can use this information to decide where to belay and how to use the remaining pieces on the rack.

Leader Responsibilities

1. Once at the anchor, the leader should get herself off belay so the second can start getting ready to move. The key to climbing fast is keeping both climbers as busy as possible. When the leader reaches the belay location, the belayer can't do anything productive until the leader calls down "Off belay." Then the belayer can take the belay device off and work on leaving the lower belay location.

2. The leader should fix the rope for the follower or put him on belay. The goal is to accomplish this before the second is ready to climb— eliminating wasted time waiting for a belay. When belaying the second, should there be slack in the line, all slack should be hauled up BEFORE the belay device is attached.

3. The leader should get the haul bag (if there is one) off the lower anchor and prepare to haul. This allows the belayer to completely take down the lower anchor.

4. If the second is climbing rather than jugging, the leader should haul the bag to the top anchor and belay at the same time.

5. The leader should set the haul bag so it is ready for the next lead.

6. The leader should be organizing the ropes and gear, placing the first pieces of the next pitch, or getting the pieces ready.

7. Finally, the leader should eat, drink, and get comfortable.

Low-angle Terrain

A lot of time is frequently lost setting up belays. While belays are crucial, it is not always necessary to have three equalized pieces. In fact, it is sometimes quite sufficient and safe to have *no* pieces in the belay at all. If the leader can drop down over an edge or crouch in between boulders, she can adequately belay a second on low-angle terrain. In this situation a hip belay can be faster and just as satisfactory.

Frequently I (B.W.) encounter this situation in the Flatirons above Boulder. Many of the climbs are fairly low-angle, and I often lead all the pitches. If I'm comfortable soloing the ground, I can run up a route much faster using this technique. A follower that falls on a low-angle slab with no slack in the rope does not put much force on the rope and can easily be held with a hip belay.

The key to moving fast isn't necessarily climbing without protection or without a belay, but being able to switch quickly from simul-soloing to simul-climbing to belayed climbing and back again based on the terrain.

Equipment

Double duty can be tricky. How do you put on the pack and tie your shoes while you are belaying the leader? How do you haul the bag and belay the second at the same time? Practice is one answer, but modern technology helps a lot as well. Using a Gri-Gri to belay allows the belayer to drop his hands from the device without the risk of dropping the climber. It is ironic that the Gri-Gri has found the most use in two widely disparate subcultures of climbing: sport climbing and speed climbing.

Rock Exotica's Wall Hauler or Petzl's Mini Traxion are also extremely handy for hauling the bag. These simple devices are light and easy to use. Combine the Gri-Gri with the Wall Hauler, and hauling and belaying simultaneously becomes a reasonable chore. The Kong Gi-Gi and the just out Petzl Reverso also allow for toprope belaying where hands-free moments do not sacrifice a safe belay.

Leading in Blocks

Climbing can be tiring, and you don't climb as fast when you're tired. You could think of climbing in the traditional manner as a series of intervals. When "swinging leads," the leader works his way up the pitch and gets to rest while the follower climbs the pitch. The follower is perhaps tired upon reaching the belay and yet has to plunge directly into the next lead. Frequently this isn't the most optimal way to climb—for speed, or even for redpointing. Also, there is a certain amount of mental preparation that goes into leading. Once a climber is in that mode, it is sometimes more efficient to stay in that mode.

Leading in blocks is a way to preserve the leader mindset and momentum and to allow the most rested climber to move. A block is a consecutive collection of pitches led by the same leader. When the Nose was first climbed in a day, it was broken up into three giant blocks; each block was assigned to the most proficient climber for the type of climbing in that block. This allowed one person to psyche up for the duties of moving the team quickly up the wall, giving his all before dropping into a supportive role. Since then, this technique has been used more often than not on speed ascents.

Both climbers should clip into the end of the rope via two locking carabiners instead of tying directly into the rope. The reason? You will switch rope ends to start each pitch that continues the same block.

How long is a block? The route and the team will dictate how the route is broken into blocks. A block might be as few as a couple pitches on a short route, or up to ten pitches on a big wall. Leading can be stressful, it can be very satisfying, and it can be both at the same time. How long a person stays in the lead will depend on a lot of factors including the following: Does the leader need a break from the stress? Has the team reached an agreed upon pitch or time allotment for the leader? Is there a good ledge to perform the switch? Has the climbing changed character, now requiring the skills of the other partner?

Belays and Changeovers

Once the leader leaves the anchor, the belayer should be moving ascenders off the rope and going direct to the anchor. The belayer's primary responsibility is to keep the leader moving. To this end, her first task should be to organize gear and ropes. Once this is done, she can start eating and drinking.

When the leader yells "Two minutes," the follower gets everything ready to jump on the ascenders or climb the pitch. If the anchor is bomber, I usually take it all down except remain clipped to one good piece. When the leader is at the top anchor and the follower is at the bottom anchor is another point when no upward progress is being made. Don't let this last long—be doing something to change it!

A classic problem happens when the top climber at the anchor yells "Off belay" and the bottom climber doesn't hear the leader. They both sit there for 15 minutes before one says, "Hey, are you climbing or what?" Be sure every verbal or signal command you give your partner gets answered. For "Off belay," answer "Okay, you're off belay." For any command ("Rope is fixed," "Bag ready to haul," etc.) at least give an "Okay" in response so that your partner knows that you heard her.

It's best to agree with your partner on set and consistent commands prior to climbing. You should use definitive words, and maybe even decide on a set number of syllables for each command. This way a garbled command will not be mistaken for a different command. Don't use "Yeah" and "Nay," instead use "Yes" and "No." If your lead partner yells "I'm off belay," don't answer "Off belay!" You're partner might think you're asking "Off belay?" There is less chance of misunderstanding if you answer "Okay, *you* are *off* belay." When you're at a busy cliff, follow all verbal communication with your partner's name. "You're off belay, Bill." Consider walkie-talkies for even better communication.

On a route when verbal communication is impossible, establish a set of "rope commands" with your partner. I have a set of rope commands that I use with all my regular partners. It never hurts to review these commands at the start of a climb. I use three sharp tugs on the rope to mean "Off belay." Two more sharp tugs on the rope means the follower is "On belay." When in doubt the second should wait for the rope to come tight to make sure he is on belay. Move up a bit (ideally still clipped to the anchors) and see if the rope becomes tight again. An important note: Only the leader uses these rope commands. The second should never pull sharply on the rope for obvious reasons.

If follower is jugging and not leading the next pitch, she should stay on the ascenders when arriving at the belay anchor and resist clipping into the anchor immediately (see Figure 2-1). Remember the goal is to get the leader moving as soon as possible. The follower just trusted their jugs the whole pitch. Why not just hang on them while the leader gets set to go?

FIGURE 2-1

Second jugs to anchor and then stays on the ascenders to swap gear, switch ends of rope, and belay for leader.

The second unclips her end of the rope, gives it to the leader, and immediately puts him on belay. Switching ends of the rope is key because the follower's end of the rope is hanging free from the belay and is ready to go immediately. There is no need to go through the sometimes complex process of unweighting the belay so that the leader can get unclipped. Also, when the second clips into the leader's end, she is already anchored to the belay. I cannot stress enough how easy and fast this makes changeovers—especially at hanging belays.

While the second is doing this, the leader can be pulling gear off the follower and arranging it on his harness or rack. These two jobs can be done by both follower and leader. Do what works best for your circumstances, but keep both of the climbers working when you're there at the anchor. It may be that the leader or follower can be still hauling while the other is racking and preparing the leader for leaving the belay. If the leader is ready to go, and the bag is not at the anchor, *and* there is little or no chance of the bag getting stuck, then the leader can start off while the belayer simultaneously hauls and belays.

Remember: When both or all the climbers are at the anchor, everyone should be doing something! This is a point where no upward progress is being made, so don't let it last long. Bust your butts to get the leader off the anchor. This is a perfect example of shaving 2 to 30 minutes off a pitch. Yes, I've seen changeovers at a hanging belay take 30 minutes or more. Feel a sense of urgency here, it won't last long. Once the leader is off and gaining altitude, there will be plenty of time for the belayer to relax, but not until the leader is on his way. Develop a set routine for belay anchor and changeover activities.

Final note: Be efficient about the gear transfer. Incidentally, most people not only call it the "hand-off" of gear, but they actually hand off the gear to each other. This is a waste of movement. Why not just clip the gear onto the leader? The leader could pull gear off you and clip it to herself, while you're also clipping gear to her, or doing something else.

Three-Person Aid Teams

Have the leader take up a trail line. When the leader arrives at the belay anchor, he should fix the ropes. When the second gets to the leader, she can take over the lead or belay the first leader on the line she just jugged. When the third climber arrives, the leader can build a quick temporary anchor and lower a loop of slack down to retrieve the other rope end and

Hans lowering out of the pendulum from Sickle to the Dolt Hole crack. (Hans Florine)

any gear cleaned from the last pitch.

If a party has three ropes, the leader can haul a bag on the third line while the two followers are jugging. The follower that is likely to get to the leader first should be bringing up the end of the trail line if they are not hauling on the third line. A pitch that might take 40 minutes or more to clean only takes five minutes to jug on a free line.

If the leader put in a ton of gear and has little or no gear left to start leading the next pitch, make sure the person jugging the free line takes any gear possible from the lower anchor and pulls out any gear along the pitch that is easy to clean. Then the leader has some gear and can continue up while you're waiting for the person cleaning the pitch below.

The free-line jugger can often remove pieces above the person cleaning the pitch, which makes the swing on traverses go easier. The opposite is true as well, clean accordingly. When a pitch is steep, consider clipping in the trail line a few times during the pitch because it is easier and faster when the follower can "drive" off the wall while jugging.

The Tis-sa-ack Story
by Greg Murphy, Bay Area climber (August 1999)

Another weekend update coming your way. This time around Chan Harrell, Peter Coward and I somehow managed to drive past El Capitan to the other big stone in Yosemite Valley—Half Dome. We reunited as "Team Pokey" to climb the historic and absolutely fantastic route Tis-sa-ack on Half Dome (VI, 5.10, A3+). We did what we believe was the first single push ascent of this route in 31 hours and 45 minutes.

We are considering a break with tradition by re-defining our particular brand of single push style as "weekend style," where a hectic work week and a long Friday night drive are mandatory elements of the ascent. As usual, it was late to the Valley on Friday night with a 3:30 A.M. alpine start on Saturday. The grueling predawn hike up 2,700 vertical feet to the base of Half Dome ensured that we were whipped before the climbing even started.

The climb takes an elegant line up the center of the huge northwest face of Half Dome. It is the most stunning climb I've ever been on—gently overhanging in its entirety and surrounded by an amazing sea of rock. Unbelievably, we were the only ones on Half Dome the whole weekend.

We started climbing at 7:15 A.M. Chan led the first block of eight pitches, while I recovered from the hike and secretly snoozed. I took over the next block as the sun hit the face. Peter, our nocturnal specialist, was kept in reserve for the graveyard shift. (Peter generally spends the entire week before the climb, the drive up, and the approach telling us that this time he is not getting the night block. Somehow, he always ends up on the sharp end when the sun goes down.)

The first fifteen pitches climbed in daylight went at a respectable pace of under one hour per pitch. As always, things deteriorated rapidly in the dark with routefinding difficulties, hard aid, questionable cleaning-while-leading tactics, unintended 50-foot pendulums, and general chaos. The next morning we cranked out the rest of the route at a somewhat slower pace and topped out in the early afternoon. The hike down was a grind and the last mile on the road seemed to take an eternity.

We decided to stay in the Valley that night instead of attempting to drive home. Peter and I tainted our weekend style ascent somewhat by not making it back to work until Monday afternoon. And Chan was unemployed but had the full-time job of dealing with prenuptial stress. This is one of the best routes around and the climbing highlight of that year.

CHAPTER 3
SPEED CLIMBING TIPS

Far better it is to dare the mighty things, to win glorious triumphs, even though heckered by failure, than to take rank with the poor spirits who neither enjoy nor suffer much, because they live in the grey twilight that knows not victory nor defeat.
—Theodore Roosevelt

Stick your neck out every once in awhile.
It's good for the soul.
—Bill Wright, our translation!

This chapter is a collection of ideas for speeding things up. The tips are in no particular order, but they are grouped together under three headings: leading, aid climbing, and cleaning. I (H.F.) have given people some speed tips in the past and invariably they'll comment on one or two of my tips by saying, "That'll only save two minutes. What's the point?" The point is that if you save two minutes at every belay on a 30-pitch route, you've cut an hour off your time on the whole route.

That hour could mean the difference between topping out when it's still light or topping out in the dark—topping out before the afternoon thunderstorms hit or getting stranded on the wall while the storm rages. Simply put, if I give people four or five "two-minute tips" for every pitch on the Nose, that'll equal around five hours saved. Five hours saved translates into one less gallon of water to be hauled, four fewer energy bars to be carried, etc. The point is that each little speed technique you master adds up.

Tips for Leading

Stay in the lead. It is strategically better (in this context that means faster) to keep the same leader throughout the whole climb. But if you must switch, leading in blocks is better than switching every pitch. Keeping the same leader means she can recover from each pitch while waiting for you to follow. She gets use to racking the gear the way she likes, and you figure out how she likes it racked. I recommend, for the sake of speed, an agreement with your partner, such as she leads all of the Nose if you get to lead all of the Salathé.

Time limit for leader. Recently Mark Melvin pointed out to me that you should consider giving each climber a set time to lead rather than dividing up pitches. Because speed climbing is about time, each climber should lead the same amount of time. So, one partner leads for three hours and the other leads for three hours. Timing your leads makes you keenly aware of your pace on the route and can help tremendously when you need to consider important decisions like retreating or pushing on. It can also quell frustration between partners of different ability/speed, in that neither will get stuck with more belay "duty."

Placing gear. When free climbing try to place gear at your chest or below. This is a good practice to use whenever you climb, including sport climbing, and it is particularly relevant to speed climbing. The gear you place won't be taking up valuable handholds, plus you won't use extra effort placing the piece high. Why bring up that loop of slack to clip in? It is a wasted action.

The tendency to place gear above your head is motivated by security. With gear above your head, you are basically toproping. In speed climbing you are quickly above the piece you just placed (or the bolt you just clipped), so the advantage of clipping above your head is reduced almost immediately after placing it. Another reason for placing gear above your head is to postpone the next placement as long as possible. This is also not as important when speed climbing because gear is usually placed farther apart.

Be smart about gear placement. Save pieces you need up high. Burn a #1 cam if you have two of them rather than using your only #2. Think of fixed gear as a free extension of your rack. Use it liberally, but realize that this gear is suspect. Fixed gear has blown out on climbers, and you need to be aware of the consequences.

After running out a long section of moderate free climbing, don't clip

Greg Murphy on a record ascent of the Shield. (Hans Florine)

into one fixed piece and start aiding. The consequences of this piece blowing out are huge. After a long runout, you need to place a solid piece, and one old copperhead is not going to do it. Once you've clipped a bomber piece, start using the fixed gear.

Favor using the fixed gear low on a lead or pitch when it is available. Higher on the pitch you can always use that cam as a draw or a cam, but draws can only be used as draws.

Your knot. Tie into the rope with the knot close to your waist, which makes it easy to keep your waist close to your high piece—an advantage when aid climbing. This also makes clipping ergonomically easier because you don't have to reach way down below your waist to grab the rope to clip. Once when I (B.W.) was on Astroman, I tied in with too much of a loop. For most of the climb, this wasn't a problem; but when I tried to follow the Harding Slot, the knot pulled up into the middle of my chest—the thickest part of my body. I was too wide to fit through the slot and ended up having to batman up outside the slot. I could have solved the problem by calling for slack so the knot would drop below my waist, but I was having problems making progress up this horribly tight passage.

Efficient movement. Certain climbing techniques are more efficient than others. When trying for speed, liebacking a crack may go faster than jamming it straight in. Liebacking is almost always quicker when ascending off-width sections. The disadvantage? It is much harder to place gear from a lieback position. Be conscious of other alternatives.

Tips for Aid Climbing

Etriers. Use four-step etriers instead of five-step. For about 95 percent of aid placements, you are *not* on the bottom step of your etrier. For the other 5 percent of the placements, just add a quick draw to the etrier to get the length. Also, use light etriers. You don't want your feet getting comfortable. You want an incentive to move. And using different color etriers helps decipher what's what in the tangle. I use red for right and lemon for left. I recently designed a pair of etriers for ABC that are light AND comfortable. (Many climbers use aid ladders instead of or in addition to etriers. Nearly all of my comments are the same for aid ladders as for etriers. We will use the term "etriers.")

Some aid leaders use two *sets* of two etriers. One set is lighter and simpler, which usually translates into speed. On very difficult aid leads and continuously overhanging terrain, there might be an advantage to having two sets. Another etrier tip: Once you've clipped the aider to the piece and bounce tested it, immediately climb to the top or second step in your etriers. Don't waste time hanging out "down low."

Aid-to-free transition. Often A3 pitches have quick and easy 5.9 moves that can save you stacks of time if you're willing to get out of your etriers. I (H.F.) have seen too many 5.12 climbers waste ten minutes fiddling with a hook or placing a nut when they could have free climbed a 5.10 move in seconds. Get used to the idea of getting in and out of your etriers. Practice making frequent transitions from aid to free climbing and back again.

If you find it difficult to step out of your aiders and bring them with you at the same time, consider leaving them behind while you free climb a section. Once above the free section, place a solid piece, lower down to retrieve the aiders, and winch yourself back up to your high point by batmanning up the other side of the side of the rope. If you bring the aiders with you, be careful that you don't step on the trailing aiders. If the aid climbing is over for the pitch, invest your time in balling up the aiders so they don't dangle down by your feet.

Wear climbing shoes. Wearing climbing shoes will always increase your speed, even if it's A5. You are *still* climbing. Don't settle into the mentality that you're just engineering your way up the wall standing in etriers. You should be constantly switching between aid and free climbing.

While climbing the Chouinard-Herbert on Sentinel Rock, my partner didn't bother to put on his climbing shoes because he thought he was only aid climbing or jugging that day. Later, on what should have been a trivial 4th class lead, he found himself making some 5.5 moves. In his climbing shoes he would have made short work of this pitch; but without the confidence provided by good shoes, he spent more than an hour leading it. Wear your climbing shoes and keep the free climber's desire to move fast.

Pin scars. When encountering pin scars, consider hand placing the pins rather than bashing them in with a hammer. Think of it as a hook move. Use a hook. Cam hooks are a godsend to speed climbers and frequently work great in pin scars. This not only saves time leading but also cleaning.

Use Black Diamond Peckers, A5 Beaks, and Pica Too-Cans like hooks in pin scars rather than pounding them in. Not only will they clean faster for the second, but the leader can clean them and often just leapfrog them up a thin section. Cams place and clean faster than nuts. When you have plenty of cams, use them before nuts even when there's a bomber V-slot.

Crack jumaring. When faced with a continuous crack, like on the headwall of the Salathé, clip a few of the appropriate pieces to the top of each etrier. Now leapfrog the etriers up the crack, like a Versa Climber. You won't need to go back searching on your rack for the next piece. This is called crack jumaring (see Figure 3-1).

FIGURE 3-1

With a continuous crack, clip a couple of cams on your etriers and leapfrog them up the crack. This is called crack jumaring.

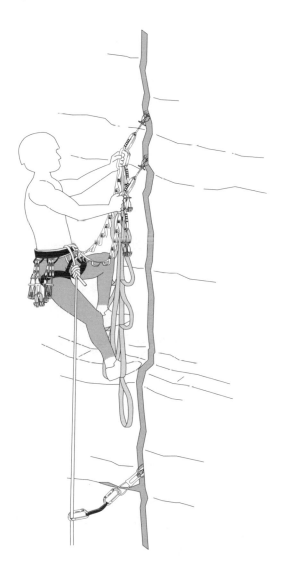

Fear versus Speed
by Chris MacNamara, Yosemite speed climber

The secret to taking two hours instead of six hours on a hard aid pitch rated A3-A5 is a matter of managing fear. The terrified climber makes slow, overly cautious movements, rarely gets higher than her third step, and often spends ten extra minutes trying to get the "perfect" placement when a fast and only slightly less secure piece would do the trick.

The speed climber, however, manages her fear and takes a much different approach. She gives each piece a solid bounce test, gets in her aiders, and marches right up to the second or top step. She realizes that once she has weighted a piece, she is committed, and there is no sense worrying about whether the piece will hold or not.

One trick she uses is to imagine that the piece, even if it appears marginal, is as bomber as a giant, ½-inch bolt, confidently telling herself, "This piece held for the last ten people, and there is no reason it is going to come out on me." Free of unnecessary fear, the movement up the pitch becomes fast, fluid, and much more fun.

Cam hooks. Become comfortable with cam hooks. Your first impression of a cam hook may be "There is no way in hell this thing will hold me." However, once you play around with them a little, you will find that these remarkable gadgets hold body weight in a variety of placements and save tons of time. On many pitches it is possible to put one cam hook on each aider and leapfrog them up long sections, saving hours of fiddling around with pitons or stoppers.

Miscellaneous Tips

1. Do not overdrive pitons.
2. To extend your reach another foot on hook placements, place the hook on top of your hammer and then slide it up the wall.
3. Create a mini-cheat stick by intertwining two stoppers together. This way you can extend your reach by one or two feet when trying to lasso rivets with no hangers.
4. Climb with lightweight biners such as the Black Diamond Neutrino or Kong Helium. This can take many pounds off a full aid rack.

Crack jumaring is moving up a crack via aiders attached to pieces of protection. Mostly the pieces of protection will be camming units because they are easier to remove after being weighted. The piece is not placed and left behind but clipped directly to the aider. Once you are standing on the top aider, you slide up the bottom aider to just below the top one, transfer your weight onto the bottom aider, and move the top one up. Leapfrogging the aiders allows for greater movement with each placement but might be more awkward than the "inchworm" approach. Use what fits the situation best.

The motion is similar to climbing a fixed line, although in practice it takes longer and can only be done efficiently with very uniform cracks (and Yosemite is particularly rich in this category). Try to keep your foot applying a little downward pressure on the aider while moving the un-weighted aider up like you were jugging a fixed line. This saves a tremendous amount of time with every movement of the aider. If you had to replace your foot in the aider each time, your speed would be cut in half.

Cleaning Tips

Racking gear. Rack gear as you clean on a sling and rack the way the leader prefers so he doesn't have to re-rack it. Just hand off the sling to the leader when you reach the belay anchor.

Clip gear on the biner with a piece that's similar in size (one biner per piece is faster). This reduces the number of times you hand gear to your partner, allows for a quick inventory of your different cam sizes, and eliminates a horizontally expanding rack (see Figure 3-2). Also, clip two or three draws together so that you can hand off more than one at a time.

Saving energy. Wait until gear is at your chest or below to remove it from the rock. Your arms tire more quickly if they are above your head.

Ascenders. Even if briefly, try to hang in your harness from ascenders rather than on your arms when cleaning a piece. This gives you a mini rest and two hands to fiddle with the gear. You will need to place ascenders above the pieces. Either unclip the piece or take the ascender off and move it above the piece. Practice taking ascenders on and off the rope with one hand.

Adjustable rack. If there is a big difference in height/size between you and your partner, it is worth having an adjustable gear sling, or a small

Grouped rack

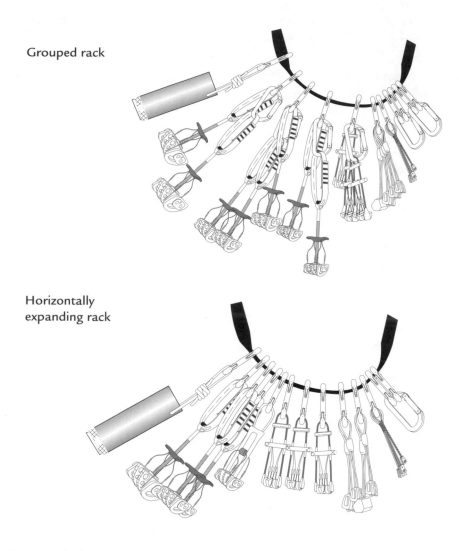

Horizontally
expanding rack

FIGURE 3-2

one and a large one. If you use an adjustable gear sling, be sure it is quick to adjust and foolproof (i.e., won't ever come undone).

Cleaning draws. When cleaning draws off a bolt, unclip from the rope first, and then the bolt hanger, so the straight gate is in your hand and ready to place on the sling, rack, or harness. Slippery hands option: Unclip from the bolt; and while the bent gate is still clipped to rope, clip the straight gate to the sling, rack, or harness, then unclip the bent gate from rope. Both methods have the same number of hand movements.

Jugging. Practice ambidextrous jugging. If you are cleaning a traverse or diagonal pitch, it is easier to be leading with the correct ascender. For example, lead with the left hand if the pitch goes left.

While jugging easy terrain on a traverse, like a 3rd class ledge, it is faster for the leader to belay you while you're on your ascenders than for you to slide your ascenders along. At the end of the traverse, the leader can re-fix the line and you can continue jugging.

Adjusting your etriers and jugging set-up. Take the time to adjust your leg stirrups or etriers under your ascenders. If the angle of the climbing is steep, you want your feet a little closer to your ascenders. If your right leg is getting tired, lengthen your right etrier, and vice versa. I designed a leg loop for jugging for ABC called a "JJ" (short for: Just for Jugging). It's a foot stirrup with an adjustable length. Metolius makes a similar item called an Easy Aider that works as well. Both eliminate the hassle of a bunch of aid ladder or etrier loops dangling around your feet while jugging. I went for years just tying a loop in a one-inch piece of webbing—also better than an etrier for jugging.

Take the time to adjust your daisy chain or tether to your ascenders from your waist. As the angle of climbing gets steeper, you want your tether length to be shorter. This is only critical on the "lead ascender" because your waist will be hanging on that ascender. The lower ascender tether should never be short enough to restrict movement.

Lower outs. If you know the route has big lower outs, bring leaver biners and a small lower out line.

Pendulums. Take your feet out of the etriers or jugging foot loops for big pendulums to keep from tripping. Forego the use of a hero loop or lower out line if the pendulum swing is low-angle and you can control your swing by smearing, edging, or running. Be sure to check that the rope won't be rubbing on an edge.

Rope management. When there isn't any potential for the rope to snag, and especially if the pitch is straight up, I will tie in short once in order to have less rope weight on the brake end when belaying the next pitch, not as a safety back up. Obviously, if the wind is blowing the rope around and it might snag, or if the terrain is subject to snagging the rope, tie in a few times as needed. Time taken organizing the rope is better than going back down to un-snag it.

Hans Florine and Chandlee Harrel on West Buttress Record Speed Ascent, a diffi-cult traversing pitch to follow. (Tom Evans)

When you belay with a Gri-Gri and then jug, leave the Gri-Gri on the rope and pull the rope down through it. Eventually the rope weight will be pulled through the device and you'll have an automatic back up behind your ascenders.

Cleaning a traverse. When cleaning a traverse, it saves time if you do not tie in short! People often recommend tying in short. I have never had a Petzl ascender *fail* on me. People *fail* to put ascenders on the rope correctly, but ascenders do not *fail*. Ascender accidents are due to improper use 99 percent of the time. So, learn to place ascenders correctly on the rope, learn it well, and then tie in short if you must!

In regard to tying in short. In general, I will always have myself connected twice to the rock or rope system. For example, if I'm tied into the rope at an anchor, the rope is tied in with at least two knots, or I'm in with one knot and a daisy chain or sling. When transferring from one rope end to another, I might momentarily only be into the anchor with a sling or daisy.

When jugging a traverse, you've been weighting both ascenders for the length of the rope below you, so essentially you've been body weight testing each ascender alternately. For a second or two, you remove one, lift it over a piece, and place it immediately back on the rope, as is the case on a traverse. You have just relied on *one* connection to the system for the time it took you to move that ascender over the piece.

Remember, the one connection you're on has been "tested" numerous times on the ascent up the rope to that point. This seems safer than what many folks do at belay anchors. I am always clipped or tied in to the end and/or the middle of the rope in addition to being clipped into the two ascenders. You should be too. So while jugging you're connected three times.

Backcountry Blasting
by Greg Murphy, Bay Area climber (July 2000)

Peter Coward and I decided that using the whole weekend to get in a long climb is extravagant, self-indulgent, and not necessary. With a little more focus, motivation, and efficiency, most climbing objectives can be completed on Saturday, leaving all of Sunday to do house projects, laundry, grocery shopping, etc. "In a day" now means leaving the house on Friday night and returning Saturday night.

In keeping with this new ethic, Peter and I drove up to Matterhorn Peak in the Sawtooth Range and climbed an outstanding route on the Incredible Hulk. This route, Astro-Hulk (5.11) was recently put up by Dave Nettle, and we may have made the second ascent. We arrived at the trailhead at 11:30 P.M. and got the alpine start going at 4:30 A.M. on Saturday. Since the birth of my second son, Alex, six weeks ago, this was a refreshingly solid five hours of sleep.

The predawn hike in was a beautiful mix of trail and cross-country, and we watched the morning sun hit the peaks above us. We did the approach in 2 hours and 23 minutes, and the elevation gain was about 3,000 feet. The face was in the shade and the first couple of pitches were quite cold.

After two warm-up pitches, the climbing started in earnest with a dicey, technical 5.11a face traverse above some roofs. Peter unlocked this section with a cool head and some smooth, devious climbing. Three more pitches of 5.10 or so took us to the stellar 7th and 8th pitches, both 5.11. Pitch 7 has some awesome clean stemming and corner turning at 5.11a, while pitch 8 climbs a striking corner with some sporty and long lieback sections between gear placements at 5.11b. Although the climb continues along the summit ridge, we opted to rap from the top of pitch 8. I had been to the summit twice before and Peter would have to wait for another day. He intends to return to do Positive Vibrations and the Red Dihedral.

We hiked out quickly and enjoyed the descent through alpine meadows and a forest of aspen and fir. The car-to-car time was 12 hours and 23 minutes, and we made it home by 11:30 P.M. The route is an outstanding mix of varied, continuous 5.10 and 5.11 climbing. The Incredible Hulk is a great destination backcountry crag with a comparatively mellow approach, a fabulous location, and a choice of great climbs.

CHAPTER 4
SIMUL-CLIMBING

God has given me the ability. The rest is up to me.
Believe. Believe. Believe.

—Billy Mills, gold medalist 1964 Tokyo Olympics

Now we get into the weird and wild stuff of real speed. When I (B.W.) first heard of these techniques they seemed radical; but now that I've used them, they don't feel so strange. Simul-climbing is definitely a new sensation, but one you might fully enjoy.

Each route will present "obstacles" that require imaginative problem-solving. For example, when the leader is lowering out, preparing for a pendulum, use the leader's weight to pull up the follower as the leader gets lowered. Be willing to break with traditional techniques if they increase speed without compromising safety.

Simul-soloing

On easy terrain, climbing unroped is an option that should be considered. Solo climbing is discussed in more detail in the next chapter. Simul-soloing is a variant of team climbing where you happen to be unroped.

You wouldn't rope up for a hiking approach, and simul-soloing is used on terrain somewhere between hiking and roped climbing. On blocky and loose terrain, often found on alpine routes, a rope can be more of a hindrance than help. Dragging a rope along such terrain merely causes rockfall.

The simple fact of the matter is that big alpine routes have a considerable amount of terrain that is best covered with this technique. George Bell, Lou Lorber, and I were able to climb the East Ridge of Mt. Temple in a single 14-hour push, not so much because of prodigious speed (it's been climbed a lot faster!), but because we simul-soloed the lower 2,000 feet, which was class 3 and 4 with some easy class 5 climbing. The level of difficulty where this technique is applicable will vary with the party, but it should be considered for covering long stretches of easy ground.

Simul-climbing

Most of the time when you're simul-climbing, you're running it out a bit. You do this because the terrain should be relatively moderate for you (otherwise you shouldn't be simul-climbing at all) and to conserve gear. The whole reason to simul-climb is so you and your partner can move at the same time. This is only valuable when climbing more than a single pitch, and simul-climbing frequently involves running many pitches together as one giant pitch. When Hans and Jim Herson set the speed record for the Regular Northwest Face of Half Dome, they simul-climbed the entire route and only restocked the leader with gear once—thereby turning a normally 24-pitch route into two pitches.

Simul-climbing can be safe. Wrong! But you can certainly reduce the danger by holding fast to some rules. Rule Number One: The bottom person has to be 100 percent. He or she can *never* fall. I (H.F.) have suffered the consequences of a bottom person fall. I survived and won't gamble like that again. *The bottom person can never fall!* (See Figure 4-1.)

Imagine standing at the base of a route that pushes your limit. Would you solo it if the only consequences were inflicted on your partner and not you? Have you ever been out on a lead, way out on a lead, say 20 or more feet? You get sketched, and you visualize what the fall will be like. Maybe you have experienced such a fall. I've had a few on steep sport routes and serious trad slabs—scary, *but* nothing compared to what will happen to you if you're only ten feet out while simul-climbing and your belayer jumps off the belay ledge, yanking you down to that last piece of pro. *Never* put yourself or your partners in a simul-climbing situation where the bottom person on the rope *might* fall.

Who's the leader? You might think "the best climber leads," just like on a traditionally belayed climb at the crux pitch. After reading the last couple paragraphs, you might reconsider and say "No, the best climber needs to go second because he absolutely can't fall." The real answer is, like so much in life, "It depends."

Yes, it is absolutely catastrophic if the second climber falls while simul-climbing, but the truth of the matter is that no one should be falling. If the odds of a fall were above 1 percent, I'd belay the pitch and not simul-climb. If one of the climbers is more experienced at routefind-

FIGURE 4-1

Consequences of the second falling can be catastrophic. The bottom person MUST NOT FALL!

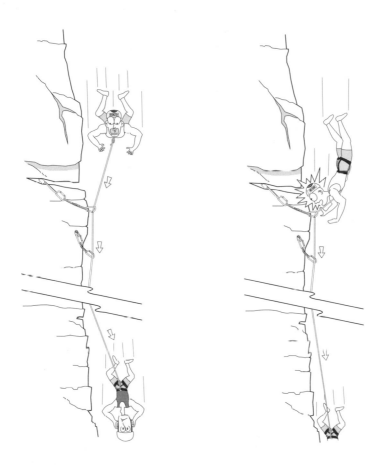

ing and placing gear, it is frequently best to have him lead. The key thing to remember is that no one can fall. Having the best climber on the bottom does slightly decrease the chances of a catastrophic fall but might negate some of the advantages of a fast leader.

Another consideration is who wants to lead. Some people are very enamored with leading. The goal of most climbing should be to have fun, so pick the leader that maximizes your fun and speed. Climbing with such a superb second is a dream. As long as the rack holds out, it is like leading on a rope of extreme length, giving you the feeling of soloing the climb without nearly as much risk.

Who Leads While Simul-climbing?

1. Who wants to lead? Who wants the greater risk?
2. Is routefinding a consideration? Who's the best routefinder on the team? Does one of the team members have the route wired? If so, she should lead.
3. Who is fastest at placing solid protection?
4. Will one climber need a real belay on a few short sections? If so, it might be best if he were to climb second so he could climb on toprope with greater confidence and hence greater speed. On the other hand, leading this section might save a belay completely because the leader climbs with a pseudo-lead belay anyway (provided the gear he places is bomber).
5. Who is best at managing the rope? Who is best at climbing with one hand? The bottom climber has the very difficult job of rope management. She must never hold up the leader's progress especially in a difficult section where the leader needs to move through it swiftly. The follower also needs to keep the slack in the rope to a minimum in case of a lead fall and be very diligent about not getting trailing loops of rope stuck.

Hans has frequently been the bottom climber on speed records. His ability to manage the rope and his vast experience with simul-climbing make him a rock solid person to "anchor" the team. (See Appendix 1 about our speed record on the Yellow Spur.) Choosing a leader depends a lot on the mentality of the climbers, the terrain being covered, and the risks each is willing to take.

The "same leader" philosophy in "pitch by pitch" leading applies here as well. It is optimum to have the same person in the lead the whole time. This creates a cycle of rest and hard work that is not interrupted by a change in the leader. The exception to this would be when the follower can literally "swing" into the lead on a big pendulum. Hans and his fastest partners do this on the King Swing on the Nose.

Guides will almost always be the first on the rope, especially when routefinding is an issue, which is a primary concern when hiring a guide. Yet on moderate terrain, guides will simul-climb with strong clients that

Hans self-belaying on Zodiac; Jacqueline (out of the picture) is cleaning the pitch; and Wayne Willoughby is organizing rope at the anchor. (Tom Evans)

they know well. Gaston Rébuffat climbed the North Face of the Dru with Réne Mallieux in such a manner. In fact, this climb provides a bit of a microcosm about why to climb fast and the joys it brings. Rébuffat describes these sensations vividly. "We had to climb fast, in fact very fast indeed, if I was to attend the guides' festival at Chamonix the next morning. This fact added zest to the whole day. To go fast merely for the sake of going fast usually seems senseless, but on this occasion it was quite different; we had only these few hours to climb the 2,500 feet of this face."

Rébuffat, like so many other climbers, had no particular love of just going fast, but once it was thrust upon him, he couldn't help but feel the joy. This experience has happened with us and the many friends we've introduced to speed climbing. They expect it to be a race, but it's not. It's moving with a sense of purpose and urgency and working together smoothly and not stopping and so much more. It is not missing out on what is great about climbing, but just enjoying a new aspect of it.

Protecting the simul-climb. If you are simul-climbing and the lower partner runs into an unsuspected jam where she needs a belay, don't let

Tiblocs and Ropemans

Folks have used Tiblocs and Ropemans to reduce the disastrous effects of the follower falling when simul-climbing. This is not an approved use of these devices. Some thought should go into their use. Be sure you put the rope "inside the carabiner" so the weight is not on the device alone in the event of a fall.

It should be noted, yet still not recommended, that the use of a Petzl Microcender or a Gibs Ascender would be safer than a Tibloc or Ropeman. Shortly after you place the ascender, it is advantageous to place a piece above it. (This is a good idea with the Tibloc or Ropeman also.) That way a fall by the leader doesn't weight the device directly but rather the higher piece. The device just lets the rope slide until the follower catches the leader. I (H.F.) don't "endorse" this, but I'm merely pointing out the best way to rig it. (See Figure 4-2).

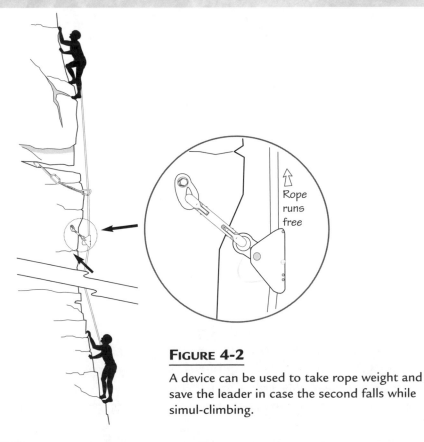

Rope
runs
free

FIGURE 4-2

A device can be used to take rope weight and save the leader in case the second falls while simul-climbing.

it throw you. Put in a temporary anchor and use it to belay her until she is past her troubles, then resume simul-climbing.

You must have pieces between you and your partner that are equal to or better than a bomber belay anchor. Three bomber pieces are a minimum. If you do not adhere to this rule, you might as well both be soloing; and if you are soloing, do not do it tied to another person. This is not glacier walking where you and your partner have ice axes and can self-arrest.

Rope selection. Some people prefer a shorter rope, say 30–40 meters, so that the climbers stay closer together in order to communicate better. Sometimes a rope shorter than standard is not an option, like when there is a rappel that is 25 meters or more. As the follower, I (H.F.) always prefer a Gri-Gri to belay, so I tend to go for a 60-meter rope because the Gri-Gri allows for a changeable rope length. (It is not correct to take your hand off the brake end of the rope when using a Gri-Gri, *but* it frees your hands up for climbing! A safer alternative is to tie a figure-8 on a bight below the Gri-Gri.)

Rope management. Do not simul-climb with huge loops of slack between you and your partner. This defeats the purpose of having a rope between you and your partner by greatly increasing the force of any fall. There are two ways to handle this problem. The first, less than ideal method, is to have both climbers climb at the same speed all the time while on each end of the rope. This can be difficult and frustrating when one climber is on a tricky section and the other is on easy ground.

The second way to handle differences in speed is by having the bottom climber use a self-locking belay device like a Gri-Gri. This allows the adept rope manager to throttle the lead line depending upon the demands of the leader and the speed of the follower. A drawback that inevitably arises from this method is that the loop of rope below the following climber can get stuck.

Communication. Good communication is always important, but even more so when simul-climbing. Make sure that you and your partner are aware of what the other is doing. I (B.W.) like to yell down "Placing a piece!" whenever I stop to put in gear. This lets my second know why the rope isn't moving. If he mistakenly thought I was at a difficult section, puzzling over the moves, he might become concerned and question why we were simul-climbing in the first place. In fact, I use this call whenever I'm climbing with my wife, Sheri. I don't want her to start worrying that

I'm dragging her up a route that is hard for me and will be very hard for her. That's not why she climbs.

Another reason to inform your partner when placing gear is that it gives her an idea of how cautious you are being. On super easy ground, the follower might be comfortable with a piece every 50 feet; and on a more difficult section, she might be happier with solid gear every 20 feet.

Finally, it is important to shut up when there is nothing that needs to be said. When someone speaks, you want the other to pay attention. This is kind of "the boy who cried wolf" application.

Simul-seconding

While simul-climbing might be a bit radical for some climbers, simul-seconding is a much safer technique that can really speed up teams of three climbers. To simul-second, it isn't the leader and the follower that are moving simultaneously, but both seconds that move together.

A traditional three-man team allows only one climber to move at a time. Hence, two-thirds of each climber's time is spent sitting at the belay. By simul-seconding, a three-man team can move as fast as a two-man team—plus offer the extra security of another member. Many people enjoy the camaraderie of actually climbing a pitch with their partner.

When simul-seconding, the leader must belay both seconds at the same time. This can be done either on a single line with both climbers tied to it, or by using two separate lines. Electing to lead on double or twin ropes is a natural in this situation and removes the dependency of the followers. If the terrain is moderate for the followers, it is not unreasonable for both of them to follow on the same line. Deciding who will be on the bottom of a single rope when simul-seconding is much simpler than deciding who will be the leader when simul-climbing. The best climber ties in to the end of the rope.

I (B.W.) remember simul-seconding on one of my early morning scrambles. My partners and I would blast in to a slab route, climb it, and then run out in time to get to work before 8 A.M. One morning Homie and I brought along Damon, a beginner climber. I led the pitch, set up a belay, and called down to Homie, the more experienced partner, "Who's climbing up next?" We had previously agreed that Homie and Damon would simul-second the rope in order to keep to our aggressive morning schedule. In his zeal to get climbing, Homie called up, "I'm going next." I tactfully responded, "Is that the best arrangement?" It only took a moment before Homie came to the same conclusion I had. It was much more likely that Damon would fall off this pitch. If Damon were the bottom climber on the rope, his weight would come directly onto Homie's harness and pull him off. I'd be fine holding both climbers, as the belay was bomber, but it would be an unnecessarily unpleasant experience for Homie. The moral of the story is that the best climber always goes last when simul-seconding.

Short-fixing

The short-fixing technique is when the leader pulls all the slack in upon arriving at an anchor and fixes the lead line so the follower can start jugging or "batmanning" the rope. Then the leader starts leading the next pitch with the extra slack in the rope—self-belaying until the second gets to the anchor. Once the second arrives, the leader is put on a standard belay, and he hauls up the gear cleaned from the second. This allows the leader to get a jump on the next pitch.

This is particularly beneficial when the pitch being followed will take a long time to clean. It gives the leader something to do while waiting for the follower to clean. Even if you are climbing at a snail's pace when on self-belay, at least you're moving up. While your partner is cleaning 100 feet of nailed pins, even the slowest leader can get in a few feet of upward movement. When the follower arrives at the fixed anchor, you can pull up the gear on a tag line, or lower a loop of slack in the lead line, to retrieve the gear from the last pitch.

This technique is really the ultimate in two people moving efficiently. You can almost eliminate the "dead time" at belays where neither team member is moving up. In an ideal ascent where the short-fixing technique is used throughout, the route the leader will always construct an anchor before running too low on gear, and will continuously assess the gear they have. If the leader knew she could only lead for another 20 feet before running out of gear, she would immediately put in an anchor and fix the rope so that she could continuing leading while the follower jugged up.

If you run out of gear, you've led too far before fixing. With this technique it is even more strategic than normal to keep the same leader the whole time. If done correctly for the whole route, the two climbers will never be at the same place at the same time anywhere on the route. Wave goodbye at the start!

Speed Record on the Salathé Wall
by Jim Herson (Summer 1999)

(Note: Three weeks prior to the adventure below, Chandlee Harrel and Jim Herson climbed the Salathé in 8 hours and 10 minutes. Then they climbed the Nose right after for a combined time of under 27 hours!)

Route selection as of late had not been all that mentally taxing, but this week was just too easy and fun. With no self-control when it comes to tweaking Greg Murphy, Chandlee and I headed back to the Yosemite "racetrack" to smoke Greg and Hans's rather pokey time on the Salathé. (Greg and Hans had climbed the route in a sluggish 7 hours and 58 minutes the week before.)

We blasted off at first light; and 6 hours and 32 minutes later, we deployed the landing chutes on top. We chopped an hour off the record (we actually climbed—aid of course—the Free Salathé, which varies at pitch 24 and 33 from the original aid line) but left plenty of fat still to trim. With a full night's sleep, reasonable temperatures, and some remedial rope handling (we got our rope stuck!), we could tidy it up into an even more respectable time. It was the most fun morning of climbing ever.

With only 24 hours left of my childhood until a purgatory of weed whacking and grouting (our house closing was that day), this trip was to be my El Cap weaning—no more than one climb up the Captain per day. But because we were an untrustworthy bunch, we had tossed in an extra sandwich and headlamp just in case. Sure enough, we hadn't coiled the rope before there was a gnawing in the pit of our stomachs from the unfinished business on the Salathé-Nose link-up. We had missed the 24 hours. (As of October 2000, this link-up has only been completed once. Peter Croft and Dave Schultz did it in 18 hours.)

We psyched up for the link-up as we sprinted down the East Ledges, then BOOM! We were whacked once again by the sizzling heat of the Valley floor. With the memory of heat stroke all too fresh from our link-up three weeks ago, we surprised ourselves and did the mature thing. A proper link-up would have to wait for a cooler day. Instead we relaxed and enjoyed the morning's memories. After all, we had already tweaked Greggie and climbing doesn't get any better than that!

CHAPTER 5

SOLOING

Speed is safety!

—Mark Twight, extreme alpinist

In this chapter we cover speed climbing techniques as they apply to soloing. This is not a complete tutorial on solo climbing. You won't find too many instructors out there who teach roped soloing. Even Long's book only has two paragraphs on this topic.

I (H.F.) have never had an instructor. I just went out and did some problem-solving. My first time out with a Silent Partner (a solo belay device), I actually had the rope clove hitched on the device improperly. I should have looked at the user manual more closely. The way I had it set up was safe, but the drag from the improper setup took five times the effort to feed out slack. I almost threw in the towel 40 minutes into my seven-hour solo ascent of the Northwest Face Regular Route on Half Dome.

Traditional Roped Soloing

To make sure we're all on the same page, I will explain traditional roped soloing (see Figure 5-1). You, the soloist, start by building a bombproof multidirectional anchor and fixing one end of the rope to it. Next you attach a solo device to the rope, such as the Wren Silent Partner or Soloist, and climb the pitch above, placing gear and clipping into the pieces. When you arrive at the next belay or anchor point, you build another anchor. Then you can rappel back down the rope to the first anchor, or you can rappel down a second line that you trailed up with you. Upon arriving at the bottom anchor, you must jug back to the top anchor, removing the gear as you go. (A second line is useful when cleaning an overhanging or traversing pitch.) Repeat this sequence until you top out. Basically, you ascend each section of rock twice, and rappel

FIGURE 5-1

Traditional Roped Soloing

Lead   Rappel   Clean

once. Fun, huh?

This may seem laborious at first; but if you work out all the ways to be efficient about it, you can move at a good pace. This traditional method of roped soloing can be used to climb even large routes quickly. I used this method when I did my first solo: the Nose of El Cap in 14 hours and 11 minutes!

Anchors. Get proficient at putting in anchors fast on any terrain. In general, I try to go the whole rope length when I'm rope soloing, ignoring the standard belay anchors. Because you're never hanging at the anchor waiting for your partner to lead or follow, it doesn't matter if it's an uncomfortable hanging belay in the middle of a pitch or a comfy ledge. Setting up and taking down anchors is the most time-consuming aspect of soloing. It's always a "dead time" because you aren't making upward progress. You want to reduce the number of times you have to do this.

There are reasons to stop on a big ledge. If you need a mental break or need to do some reorganization, a ledge might be just the thing. The gear on your rack also dictates your stopping point. You may have to stop before the end of the rope, and you don't have that option to simul-climb while soloing. However, you do carry the end of the rope with you, so you'll know when to stretch it that extra ten feet and when to throw in an anchor five feet below.

Carrying gear. You want to move as efficiently as possible. When you are leading, don't carry anything you don't need. Weight kills your speed; and with the complexity of a solo system, reducing weight is extremely important. Gear that is useless on lead includes the ascenders, backpack, wide gear (if it's a thin lead), extra water, and haul bag (if you've got one). You can bring all this stuff when you're on ascenders, going up the pitch the second time.

When rapping the pitch don't bring anything down with you that you don't need at the bottom anchor. You'll just have to carry it back up the pitch. You don't want to fight gravity any more than you have to. Leave the Silent Partner, the rack of gear, and any remaining water at the top anchor when rapping down to clean the pitch.

Also, don't clean when you rappel! Clean on the way up. Why carry it down to the bottom anchor and back up? Some tricky pendulum traverses are exceptions. When you rappel a traverse, like the Great Roof Pitch on the Nose, you'll need to decide if you want to follow the line of the route when you jug or clean on the way down and do one big lower out at the bottom of the pitch. Different situations will dictate different answers.

Rappelling the pitch. If you are using a Gri-Gri for soloing, it is probably also your lowering device. If you are using a solo belay device that is not convenient for descending, such as a Silent Partner, leave it at the top still rigged for leading so you can clip back into it and take off after you've cleaned the pitch (see Figure 5-2). Simply clip into the Silent Partner and unclip the knot labeled A. This technique only works if you are at the end of the rope when you arrive at the anchor. And it will be a little tricky on natural pro when you're switching from an anchor set up for jugging to an anchor that may have to hold the upward pull of a lead fall. Use your judgment to find a way to quickly reconfigure the anchor so you can lead off of it.

FIGURE 5-2

Rappelling the pitch

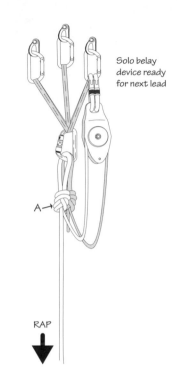

Solo belay device ready for next lead

A→

RAP

Traversing. Let's start with a scenario where you don't have a trail line (see Figure 5-3). If you're going to follow the line of the route on a traverse, lowering from the anchor (far right in diagram) and going "left" past each piece, try this trick: When you near the first piece, clip into it behind the rope with your daisy chain (frame 1); then lower enough so all your weight is on it (frame 2). Next, unclip the rope from the piece (frame 3). Re-clip the rope coming from the anchor in above you and get your weight on the rap device (a Gri-Gri is nice for this). Finally, unclip your daisy from the piece where you are and clip it into the next piece to the "left" (frame 4). Repeat this process at each piece.

If you have a trail line, the best way to tackle a traverse is different. Imagine a low-angle wall where the bottom anchor of a 200-foot pitch is only 20 feet right of the top anchor. If you clean on the way down, you have one easy swing out at the bottom, then it's just haul ass jugging a straight line back to the top anchor. If the same anchor setup was on a 5-, 10-, or 20-degree overhanging wall, I'd leave the pieces in and the rope clipped into them for the jug back up. It's easier and faster to jug on a steep wall when you can drive off the wall than when you're dangling in the air ten feet away from the wall.

Whenever there is a large pendulum, especially off an established

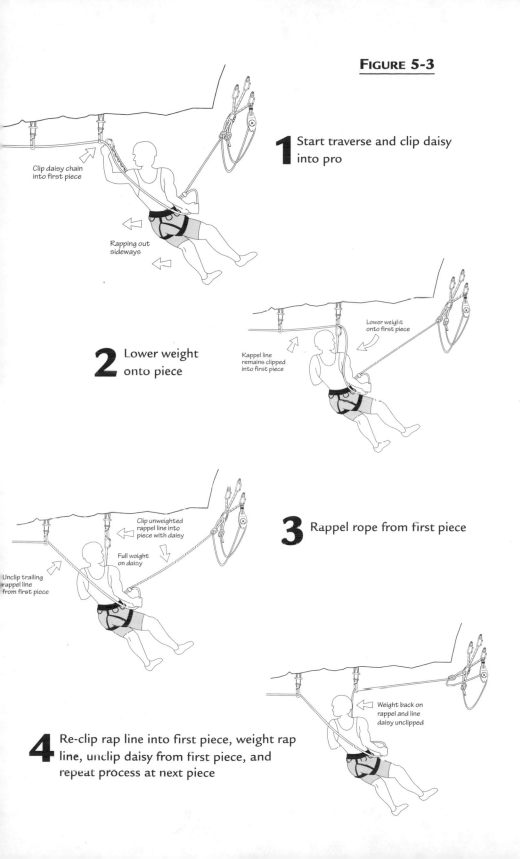

FIGURE 5-3

1 Start traverse and clip daisy into pro

Clip daisy chain into first piece

Rapping out sideways

2 Lower weight onto piece

Lower weight onto first piece

Rappel line remains clipped into first piece

3 Rappel rope from first piece

Clip unweighted rappel line into piece with daisy

Full weight on daisy

Unclip trailing rappel line from first piece

4 Re-clip rap line into first piece, weight rap line, unclip daisy from first piece, and repeat process at next piece

Weight back on rappel and line daisy unclipped

anchor with a rap ring or leaver biner, consider lowering off it with all your stuff. Make the swing, build another anchor, and pull the rope. Cool! You don't have to backtrack that pendulum!

There are more things to consider in regards to traversing. More than I can address here—angle of the wall, sharpness of the traverse, and ability of the climber, to name a few. There are other ways to deal with a trail line and without a trail line. Use your imagination and apply some of the techniques discussed here. Each situation is unique. The idea is to make your efforts produce the most efficient and fastest way through the obstacle course.

Trail line tip. A trail line is useful for hauling and emergency retreat whether you're soloing or not. Here is a tip to consider if you don't have a partner. A fifi hook can be used to facilitate solo hauling. When the pitch is straight up and down, set up the haul bag on the trail line with a fifi hook so you can haul before you clean the pitch. If the haul bag gets stuck, you can free it when you go down to clean (see Figure 5-4). Obviously if you've led a traverse pitch, just rap the trail line, hook the bag to the bottom and lower it out, clean the pitch, and then haul. If you're not hauling, a trail line can be used as a backup and for jugging the pitch with a pack on.

Handling rope weight. When soloing, climbers complain about the rope weight that they have to deal with. Knots on your pieces are used to take rope weight and facilitate rappelling to clean (see Figure 5-5). Once or twice during

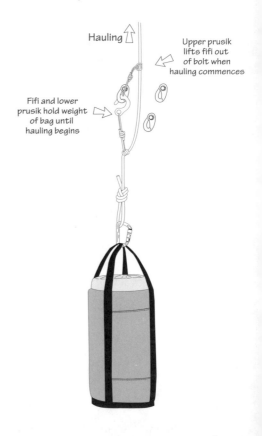

FIGURE 5-4

Trail line tip

Hauling

Upper prusik lifts fifi out of bolt when hauling commences

Fifi and lower prusik hold weight of bag until hauling begins a lead, I fix the rope to a good piece. (Note: This is not great when you fall because you don't make use of the full dynamic stretch of the rope.) Fixing the rope takes all the weight of the rope below that piece off of you. It can also keep the rope from abrading over edges both on the jug up and if you fall on lead. If you tie off occasionally, by the time you're on the last part of your solo lead, you'll have almost zero rope weight. Remember that when you solo, there is never any rope drag, so long runners are rarely needed. Compare this to a leader with a belayer who has nearly the entire weight of the rope and tons of rope drag at the end of a long lead! Now stop complaining.

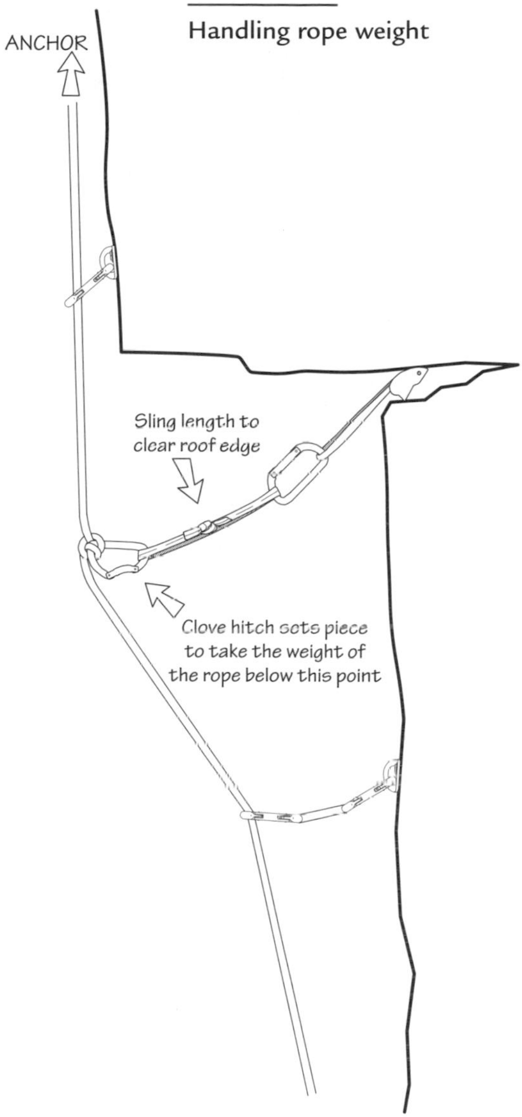

Rope management. Be careful with your rope management when you solo (see Figure 5-6). In normal lead climbing you are tied in to a single rope; but when you rope solo, there are at least two ropes, and usually three or more, trailing down from your waist. It can be confusing, and you have to get used to it. The Silent Partner, as well as other solo devices, will

FIGURE 5-5

Handling rope weight

ANCHOR

Sling length to clear roof edge

Clove hitch sets piece to take the weight of the rope below this point

feed better or worse with less or more rope hanging from them. You'll learn the right amount for *you* with experimentation.

With the Silent Partner, I'll usually have the rope tied in only at the halfway point when I leave the belay anchor. (Wren recommends backing up the device every 30 feet.) When I've led up half the length of the rope,

FIGURE 5-6

Be careful with your rope management when you solo!

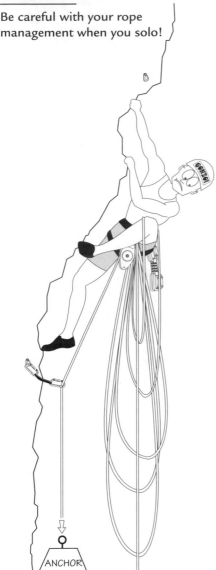

ANCHOR

I re-tie in so that there is about 20 feet of the end of the rope remaining, plus the new loop I've created. Some people re-stack their rope at each anchor in a rope bag and take it along with them. This is a great idea when the wind is bad and/or there are tons of flakes for the rope to get snagged or cut on.

Non-traditional use of rope when soloing. Just because you are soloing and you have a rope, doesn't mean you have to use the rope in a traditional manner (see Figure 5-7). A few times when there have been some bomber rap rings, sturdy slings, or leaver biners, I've threaded through and "self-belayed" off of that piece or anchor. Then I climb along and don't put in any pro. When I get to a safe anchor or have built an anchor, I just pull the rope like after a rappel. I don't have to go back at all! Dean Potter used this technique on virtually the whole length of the routes when he soloed El Cap and Half Dome in a day.

Often you might rely on the two daisy chains you're connected to as your sole means of safety, basically "French free soloing." You may occasionally loop the rope through a bomber fixed or "leaver" piece as you go by, then pull the rope when you reach the next fixed or "leaver" piece. This is a tenuous situation; remember you are relying on your pieces not to blow, or maybe even your handhold sometimes. Ask yourself "If things fail, will falling back 10, 20, 30 feet or more to the leaver piece be an option?" On trade routes in Yosemite, the fixed pieces can be

FIGURE 5-7

Non-traditional use of rope

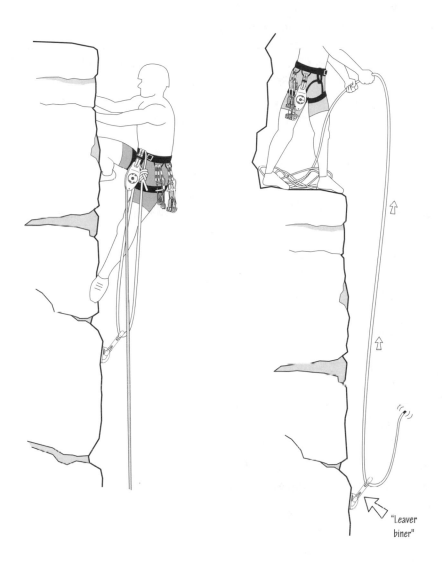

"Leaver biner"

plentiful, but leaver biners could get expensive. (Obviously you can thread through slings as well.) Russel Metrovich basically just "French free soloed" all of the Zodiac, or "aid soloed" on his daisy chains. The salutation of Greg Murphy strikes me here: "Go fast. Take chances."

Unroped Soloing

Bill and I both enjoy unroped climbing but do it at a level far below our onsight ability (at least five number grades below for Bill, and usually more). Other climbers are quite comfortable closer to their limit. Derek Hersey, the legendary Colorado free soloist, would routinely free solo routes up to 5.11c when his onsight ability was 5.12a—a difference of only two letter grades. Hersey would onsight solo up to 5.11a! Peter Croft regularly soloed routes up to 5.12a and Dean Potter once soloed a 5.13 sport route.

It seems that the best speed climbers can't help but be drawn toward unroped soloing. Nothing limits their speed. Some of the foremost soloists have also been the premier speed climbers. John Bachar, the first to envision and then climb El Capitan and Half Dome in the same day, is still legendary for his bold solos of up to 5.12c. Croft shocked the world with his amazing solos, including the first solo of Astroman. He also climbed El Capitan and Half Dome in a day with Bachar. Later with Dave Schultz, Croft became part of the only team to climb both the Nose and the Salathé in a single day. Potter's bold extension of the speed climbing game was to combine unroped free soloing with speed ascents of the biggest walls.

Soloing is an individual decision, and it can be addicting. After soloing the Casual Route on the

Great Roof Pitch: the Nose. (Steve Schneider)

Diamond, Roger Briggs, noted Colorado speed climber, said he wouldn't do anymore. He was afraid he'd like it too much. Derek Hersey, who once soloed three routes of 5.10 and 5.11 on the Diamond in a single day, fell to his death on the relatively easy Steck-Salathé in Yosemite. He was one of the world's best soloists and climbing on what was, to him, easy terrain. As they used to say on *Hill Street Blues* "Let's be careful out there."

Unroped soloing is such a pleasant and unencumbered experience. All the bothers of gear, ropes, anchors, belaying, and rappelling are stripped away; all that's left is climbing. Bouldering shares this appeal, but most problems happen low enough to the ground to permit you to safely jump off. Soloing is a different story. Obviously, the climbing must be within your "no fall" range. People vary widely on the terrain they are willing to solo, and many great climbers won't even solo the most trivial climbs. The reward to risk ratio is not high enough to justify the venture for them.

I don't have any tips for going fast when unroped soloing. The simple fact that you are unroped is enough, no? One philosophical note: If you feel you "must" free solo fast, ask yourself "Why am I doing this?"

Vision, Failure, and Triumph on El Capitan
by Steve Schneider

In California's Yosemite Park California, there is a world-famous rock known as El Capitan. One of my first memories of El Cap was during a family vacation to Yosemite when I was eight years old. My oldest brother Bob was climbing a route on El Capitan; and I tried to see him, but he was too far away. Then there was this big rescue for some guy on the Nose. I could see the rescuers lowering down the 1,000-meter face.

My mom was worried that it might be my brother who had gotten hurt, but it also seemed like she was proud to be worried because, after all, that was her son climbing that huge wall. Not only did my brother come through unscathed, but he got to ride in the helicopter because he helped carry big ropes for the rescue. His motto for that climb was "Five days up, five minutes down."

I followed in my brother's footsteps and did the Nose 11 years later, having prepared by climbing several Yosemite big walls. The year was 1979. Four years prior the Nose had been climbed in a single day by legendary climbing figures. My partner, Stan Miller, and I remarked how phenomenal that was because we were climbing it in three and a half days. It seemed incredible to climb that fast. A few years later I came back and climbed the Nose with Karl McConachie in just over 10 hours. Somehow through determination and effort, I had become one of Yosemite's fastest climbers.

For some reason I got it into my head that I had to solo the Nose in a day. Several big-name climbers had tried, but nobody even got close. It was one of the biggest prizes in the Valley, and I felt it was my destiny to accomplish this stunning feat. On my first attempt I failed mostly because I could not find an efficient method to belay myself. Leaving the ground at midnight, I arrived over 20 hours later on Camp VI—a descent ledge 600 feet from the top. I didn't have enough hours left on the 24 hour clock to finish the climb.

Demoralized by my failure and completely exhausted physically and mentally, I decided to bivy. I never slept. The cold crept into my body, which caused me to shiver and my legs to cramp—it was altogether quite miserable. The next morning I thought about retreating but didn't want to quit what I had started. I summitted about 37 hours after starting the climb, which sounded pretty good after I thought about it. It sure was hard to climb El Cap solo, but it was also extremely satisfying. It was the first climb I ever rope soloed.

Some years went by and I forgot about the pain and suffering of the attempt. In the meantime my friend Mark Blanchard, inspired by my attempt and a genius at metal work, made a self-belay device called the Silent Partner that promised efficiency and safety. I checked it out and decided to give the Nose another try. Nobody had soloed it in a day yet.

On my second attempt, everything worked great, especially the Silent Partner. I was at about the same fitness level as last time but made faster progress. The Nose is about 34 pitches in length, so I had to average about 42 minutes a pitch. One strategy I employed was to start at 5 P.M. I would be rested and climb the first section with daylight. Then I would climb after dark while I was fresh and moving well. On my previous attempt I learned that climbing at night was not much fun when you are exhausted.

On El Cap Tower, nearly halfway up the climb, I reasoned that I would probably make it if I did not get too dehydrated. Committing to go light and fast, I opted to carry less than one gallon of water. On Camp V, I got lucky and found some water—not a lot, but enough to just make me comfortable.

The summit wasn't far ahead, and I still felt good. As I got closer, I got tired and excited at the same time. The prize of being the first person to solo the Nose in a day gave me new reserves of energy. I ended up with a time of 21:22:20. I measured from when I started climbing the first pitch to when I finished following the final pitch. I had done it—the prize was mine.

I really liked the feeling of digging deep within myself for more energy in the face of extreme fatigue. When I found that my inner strength was as strong as the task before it, I had a feeling of strength in my entire life. At the same time I thought about how big a climb it was for me and realized how small I am in the real world—next to the bulk of Mother Nature.

A few years later my best friend, Hans Florine, soloed the Nose in under 15 hours. At first I was a little saddened that he broke my record so convincingly. He looked at me with his pretty blue eyes and pointed out that we were the only two people in the world to have soloed the Nose in a day. That sounded like we were in an exclusive club of two, and I was happy again.

CHAPTER 6
THE ART OF PASSING

What is the proper way to pass another team? I (H.F.) always figure the team ahead has the power to say "Yeah" or "Nay." They have dibs on the route because they got on it first. Whether you agree with this or not, is no matter. Always let the party you want to pass know that you are *asking* them if you can pass. Simply by asking rather than demanding, you have empowered them. They feel good about it, and everyone knows where things stand. It's your job to be pleasant and seek their permission to pass. Setting up things this way has never failed me. It just never hurts, and almost always helps, to be nice, cheerful, and polite. Having the attitude that you're going to pass no matter what is certainly not the way to start things. Respect other climbers and don't give speed climbers, or yourself, a bad name.

When you are coming up on a slow party, take a breather before you reach them. Then climb confidently, in control, and quickly up to them. By closing the gap on them fast, they are more likely to see how little you would slow them down if they let you pass. Look for alternatives to the route that would allow you to go around the other party without inhibiting their climbing. Plan your breaks, if you take any, so that you can pass in an easy place, like a huge ledge.

Choosing to pass a party that is at a belay anchor is obvious. Look at where your ropes are and where they will be, then lead over, through, or around accordingly. Passing people while they are on lead, or while one member is at a higher belay anchor, may involve clipping into or over their gear. Ask the other party if this is okay. If you don't ask, you might spook the leader and cause them to fall *on you!* Always ask first!

I only clip another climber's gear if it is clipped to a fixed piece like a piton, and there is no chance of clipping through the fixed piece. If they have a 1-inch cam in the crack, I place another 1-inch piece next to it. There are too many bad things that can happen when you clip someone else's gear. Avoid it, not only for style or ethics, but for logistics and safety.

Hans passes two Koreans just after King Swing. (Tom Evans)

Consider imaginative solutions to passing. I went up the Zodiac recently and ran into a Spanish speaking team from Basque. (Mi Espanol es muy malo!) Their leader was just finishing a long lead, and the cleaning was going to be time consuming. I offered to clean their gear while I led, and then I had their second jug a free line. Instead of waiting for my follower to clean my lead, the Basque team let me borrow their gear for the next lead, and I hopped right to it. We fixed their line on the pitch above as a "trade" for letting us climb through. (Techniques like this work great but might invalidate a speed record. See Chapter 11.)

I've come across slower parties and handed them a Camalot or some biners or an etrier that they had left or gotten stuck a few pitches below. This surely bought me some goodwill, which makes passing a bunch easier. I've also fixed the rope on more than one occasion for people that let me pass. In the end, they got off the rock anywhere from 30 minutes to 4 hours faster.

Never use the argument that a party should let you pass because you are going for a speed record. Don't try "I have no bivy gear" in order to get someone to let you pass, or whine that you only prepared to be out for ten hours. They'll just think you're pompous or unprepared or stupid.

Hans and Jim on the Regular Northwest Face, Round One (or "Lefty on Half Dome")

by Hans Florine (September 1999)

Well, Jim Herson and I were planning to do the Regular Northwest Face (RNWF) on Half Dome and then go for some fun free climbing on the Zebra après speed. Jim came out to my home at a respectable hour on Saturday evening, and we had the rack ready and food devoured long before 10 P.M.—albeit an incredible haggling match over the number of runners and biners to bring. Geez, the guy wanted to bring 50 runners! I did talk him down to 15 runners and 10 draws. I thought for sure we'd get to the base and he'd pull out 40 saying, "Oh look, I forgot these were in the bottom of my pack. Guess we might as well take them along!"

Getting to bed before 11 P.M., I figured there would be no praise for us doing a big day on limited sleep. Jim's idea of an early start time is 9 A.M. I talked him into a 6 A.M. wake-up. I heard strange noises at 3 A.M. and shook it off as some vagabond climber dropping in after a long Saturday wall. When I went to wake up Jim, he grimaced. He was up half the night not able to sleep until just before I woke him. At his request, we put off the wake-up for two more hours. We left the stables parking lot at 8:24 A.M., and despite Jim's lack of enthusiasm toward setting a hiking record, we made it to the base in a respectable 1 hour and 57 minutes.

Now we were at the base—time to flake the rope and gear up. I heard that Jim was anal about his shoes, so I was prepared to see two types of climbing shoes come out of his pack, presumably one pair for the Zebra free climbing and a comfy pair for the Regular Route. Jim informed me that he had left one pair in the trunk at the last minute because our start was so late that he figured he wouldn't need the Zebra free climbing shoes. I was a little perplexed when I saw two different types of shoes coming out of his pack. Jim started cursing this and that and apologizing as if he'd forgotten the rack. Then I saw that he definitely had two types of shoes, and they were both *lefties*! One left Boreal Ballet and one left Boreal Laser!

After numerous rounds of self-abasement, the realization that

Greg Murphy would never let him live this down, and various offers to keep me silent, Jim was finally ready to discuss the options. Common sense, and my dislike for the hike into Half Dome, dictated that we climb the route anyway and try to have fun. There's a novel thought.

So with a left Ballet and a right sole-flapping approach shoe, Jim set off on lead. I never was within physical-touching range of him until the summit blocks 2 hours and 25 minutes later! Despite missing the record, we had a hell of a fun time. Not bad considering Jim said he might lower down after the first pitch if he wasn't having fun. We passed five parties, two of which were doing the route in a day.

I figured I should try for another record once on top—the descent of the cable handrail on the backside of Half Dome. (I remembered to stop the watch at the bottom this time.) The time to beat: 2 minutes and 23 seconds. I time from the top huge eye bolt anchoring the cable in the granite to the same on the bottom. Needless to say, Jim didn't come up with an offer to keep me silent. Don't be too hard on him, Greg and company; he may just have you on belay in the near future.

CHAPTER 7
GEAR SELECTION AND RANDOM TIPS

How much gear do you bring? Is light right? In some cases, Yes! If you've done a route before and you know what pieces you need, choosing the gear to bring is a cinch. Our friend, Greg Opland, has climbed the Mace, a classic Arizona desert tower, 13 times. He has reduced his rack for this five-pitch route to just six pieces of gear by virtue of his experience on this route.

If you're strong on hand jams, you might consider *not* taking (or taking fewer) hand jam size pieces, and the same logic goes for finger- or fist-sized cracks. If you're making the rack for someone else to lead, consider their strengths and weaknesses. Remember, the more gear you take, the longer you can lead before having to stop and belay. Of course, more gear is more weight and that can lead to an unmanageable and detrimental amount at some point.

When you're climbing in an alpine environment, take a large selection of stoppers and hexes—rather than cams. The stoppers and hexes are lighter and cheaper, good if you have to leave them behind, as is often required in alpine adventures.

As with any leading, be imaginative about protection. Remember that a nut can be turned on its side to fit two sizes of cracks. A nut can also be used as a rivet hanger and a quick draw.

Clothing

This is an extremely place-, speed-, and time-dependent subject. Choose your clothing based on where you are, your expected speed, and the time of year. In Yosemite you can go from shorts and no shirt to a down jacket with layers of fleece underneath and a Gore-Tex shell over it all in the same day. Ask the locals in the area what to wear, that's the best bet. The big thing to remember is that "movement equals heat," and you're moving a lot, hopefully, when you're speed climbing.

Jim and Hans on the Regular Northwest Face, Round Two (or "Sling Diplomacy")

by Jim Herson (October 1999)

Climbing with Hans Florine is not unlike touring the Louvre in a bullet train. It is not the alpine, solitary, and contemplative retreat you might expect. Nor is it the spiritual experience big wallers painstakingly undergo as doubt, fear, and self-pity give way to confidence, courage, and self-pity. No, climbing with Hans is to flaunt contempt for the length, difficulty, and historic significance of the Valley's tallest. Gosh, is it fun!

Embarking on a mission that made Albright's Middle East shuttle diplomacy look like umpiring a little league scrimmage, Hans and I returned to the negotiating table to explore a framework for that seemingly intractable sling thing. For those not familiar with the religious fervor ignited by this thorny issue, it seems Hans, the big stud muffin, can't be burdened to climb with an extra six grams of nylon webbing! Unfortunately, I've grown much too proficient at coddling these overgrown, high maintenance, needy partners (Hi Greg, Chan, Peter, Jeff!). You can't just silence them with a plate of grub (Hi Allen, Chris, Jacques!) or cheap red wine (Hi Ann!). You have to give, give, give and only then hope their whining subsides. My daughter, Kara, can't be weaned soon enough so dad gets back his number one partner—who, I might add, enthusiastically defers to *all* my climbing and gear brainstorms!

Anyway, all I could squeeze out of Hans, the Netanyahu of sling negotiations, was a meager two slings per pitch for the pitches we planned to link. In exchange I had to forfeit the aiders. Also, rather than catch more flack for thinking outside the box, I decided, at the cost of great personal discomfort, to wear both left and right climbing shoes this round.

After meticulously preparing the perfect Half Dome rack—about 50 items including slings, biners, and cams—I gave Hans a Gri-Gri and a quart of water to carry. He remembered to bring one of them. Ironically, on my first trip up the Dome, one of my partners, who is also very tall, long-haired, goofy, and blond, shortchanged me on water (Hi Dave!).

Just as Royal Robbins and company might have done 40 years ago had they thought to pack more slings, Hans and I fired the Regular Route in a zippy 1:53:25. I led the route as one pitch, breaking stride once in mid-pendulum on the Robbin's Traverse to spruce up the rack. Whatever headaches he caused in packing, the king of speed more than made up for with the perfect, cushy belay. Batting cleanup on these simul-climbs is best left for the master. Not only is falling *not* an option, but you have to constantly throttle the lead rope using the Gri-Gri, making sure never to slow the leader when he's on easy ground and keeping minimal slack in the system at all times. No matter how hard I tried, I couldn't shake that blond maniac at the end of the rope, yet I didn't get hosed once! And, he quickly dispatched with the two (inevitable) rope snags. (On slow sections the second catches the first leaving long loops of rope hanging.) Nice work Hansy!

Other than one small Tibloc mishap that almost left me in a foul mood (a Tibloc isn't designed and should *never* be used for simul-climbing—'nuff said), the climb was a blast! We blazed up to Big Sandy in 1 hour and 15 minutes. I lost a few minutes in the Zigzags because I was short a few draws (which I left at the one gear exchange—doh!) and had to back clean and conserve gear. We finished the route with a hip belay just like Robbins and company must have done 40 years ago.

We speculated that this was the first sub-two-hour grade VI, which is weird if you consider that a grade VI is defined as any climb longer than, say err, two hours! Anyway, having now climbed a total of 48 pitches together in a bit over 4 hours, Hans and I have yet to share a belay. He still has no idea I can't tie a cordelette.

Jacqueline Adams, Beth Rodden, and I were on a three-day outing on the Nose in March. For above the waist we brought T-shirts, light long-sleeve tops, a fleece jacket, and a shell. For below the waist we brought shorts and long fleece pants. One of us had shell pants. We froze are buns off! It was the coldest trip I've ever had up El Cap! When Peter Croft and I climbed the Nose on El Cap in a day, we both started with shorts and T-shirts. He threw off his shirt after the first pitch. We were plenty warm the whole way up!

Gearing up for the Salathé Wall. (Tom Frost Collection)

Random Tips

Clove hitch. Use a clove hitch (instead of a figure-8) to tie in to the anchor because it is easier to manipulate your hanging position than an eight. The clove hitch also tends to be easier to undo after it has been weighted. If you clove to the "high piece" at the anchor, you'll be ready to undo it and put yourself through it for the next lead, assuming you're leading the next pitch (see Figure 7-1).

Fixed gear. Call out when you've clipped a fixed nut or fixed cam to alert your partner so he doesn't waste too much time trying to remove it.

FIGURE 7-1

Leader cloved into high piece and ready to take off.

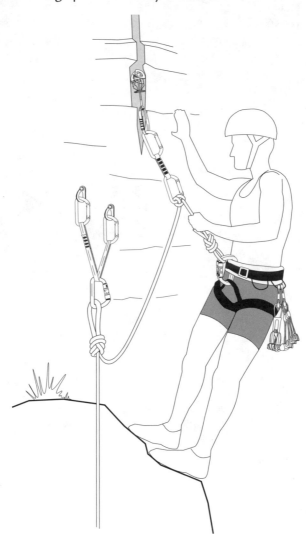

Transferring gear. Do *not* take gear off yourself and clip it to the anchor because then your partner has to grab it again and clip it to herself. Reduce duplication of work! Have your partner take it right off you and clip it where she wants, or hand the gear to your partner directly.

Approaches. When running or hiking on approaches or descents, clip the biners on your cams to the cam end of the unit so they don't swing around and hit you. On big cams there is usually biner-sized holes on the camming section to clip to. On TCUs you can just clip over the end cables between the end shaft and the trigger. For other cams be creative and find ways to keep them from swinging around. Clip the biners on your quick draws together to prevent excessive flopping.

Rope. Mark the halfway point in your rope. This saves untold time on rappels and in other situations.

Belay device. Always put your belay device in the same place on your harness or rack. That way you'll never have to search for it. The same goes for your nut cleaning tool and other regularly used items.

Simul-rapping. Consider simul-rapping when rap anchors are bombproof. Clip your partner to your rappel device with a two- to four-foot sling or daisy chain, then rap down in tandem. The other option is for each of you to rap on opposite sides of the rope. Clip into your partner with a three- to five-foot sling or daisy chain. This keeps you and your partner within reach of each other. I recommend using a block under your rap device in case either climber lets go of the brake end.

Partners. Climbing with different partners can introduce you to new (often faster) ways of doing things. You need to be discriminating about your partners, of course, but always be open to learning something. Make an effort to safely experiment with new methods.

Anchors. If you're out of cordelettes or slings, simply tie in to each anchor piece with the rope. Leaving some slack between the anchor points allows you to make an equalized "master point," just like a cordelette.

How-to books. Read a variety of "how-to" books. I like the manual put out by the American Mountain Guide Association (AMGA). I'm not an AMGA guide. Many basic systems can be illustrated well in a book. Simple tricks of the trade can be revolutionary to you, and me, when you discover how to apply them in some time-saving way.

Night climbing. When night climbing, use a halogen bulb. You can lose a lot of time if you don't know where you are going. A good light will help you see features on the route. It's nice to have a dual headlamp, one with a regular bulb as well, so you can conserve battery power when you don't need to see past your immediate surroundings. There are now a variety of small LED headlamps to choose from, and many of them last for longer than a hundred hours. I highly recommend getting one. They're so small that there is no reason not to keep one in your pack or clipped on the back of your harness.

Link-ups. Take time to plan ahead when considering link-ups of multiple routes. Where will you leave your packs? How will you avoid excessive elevation gain and loss between routes. What are some of the sun/shade variables? Time spent on logistics beforehand can save you hours of extra work on the day of your link-up.

When rapping down a gully, or terrain where rope snags are possible, it is often better to rap twice with one full-length rope, than to rap once with two full-length ropes tied together. If you have two ropes, have the first person down take the second rope with them and have them set up the second rappel while the second and/or third climbers are rapping the first line. When there are multiple rappels in a row continue to "leapfrog" the ropes down to the bottom so that they can be used on the bottom rappel.

CHAPTER 8
FOOD AND WATER

If you're hungry, it's already too late to eat. If you're thirsty, it's already too late to drink. You won't die, of course, but your performance has already diminished, and that's important. This chapter stresses simple steps to proper fueling for a high output effort. Keep in mind that everyone's body responds differently to temperatures and altitudes. Also, your body will respond differently at different times in your life. There are many good books written about nutrition for sports performance.

When to Eat

If a route will take me less than two hours, I usually go light with no food except for what is in my stomach. You can't carry all the food energy you'll need in your stomach if you're going for a 24-hour push. I recommend many small meals during a long push rather than a few big meals. I try to eat a Power Gel or the equivalent (110 calories, 28 carbohydrates) every 80 minutes (I weigh 155 pounds). When it's really cold or you are sitting at a belay in chilly temperatures, you will need more energy to keep warm. When it's really warm or you are moving pretty fast and sweating, you will need to fuel that movement and replace the fluid loss.

I often eat when I am not hungry. I eat based on time, temperature, and movement. Sometimes I eat simply because I can, like when I am belaying a long lead or waiting for the follower to jug up. I try to never stop the upward movement of the team in order to eat.

I (B.W.) used to pride myself on how long I could go without eating. I'd go cragging all day long and never stop for lunch. My partners would always need to stop and refuel. While it is certainly nice to be able to draw on such resources, this is not the way to perform at your peak over a long period of time. If I had eaten more on these days, I would have had even more energy, climbed even better, and moved even faster. The primary reason I didn't eat was that I didn't want to stop climbing. Well, you can have both. The key is to eat on the approach, while belaying, and whenever you're not doing something else.

Given nice temperatures when I'm moving slowly like on hard aid, I (H.F.) might eat less frequently. When I have just stuffed my face at the base of a route with a King Pin Apple Fritter, I might wait longer than an hour and a half before I start nibbling on my first mini meal. If I have less than an hour and a half of climbing left to the top and I'm feeling strong, I might opt to not use blood supply for digesting of the last mini meal and save it for the top. When you eat, blood goes to your stomach and intestines to transport nutrients to the body and is "taken away" from its task of bolstering the ATP process in the muscles—say in your forearms—and "fueling" the muscle activity.

What to Eat

Variety is key. Choose a variety of things to eat for long pushes. Frequently when you get tired or are at high altitudes, you lose your appetite; and of course, this is the worst thing that can happen. You eat so you don't bonk. If you bonk, your performance is diminished and it will take you longer to recover.

Give yourself every advantage by bringing a mixture of foods so that you increase your chances of finding something desirable. It's easy to bring along a few different foods so that eating is more pleasurable. Mix it up—try different flavors of power bars and gel packets and an assortment of trail snacks. Bring a bagel and maybe a yam, even an apple—although you don't get that much energy from an apple, they are wet, and more importantly, they are *different*!

For an eight-hour push on a 75-degree Yosemite day half in sun and half in shade, I would first be sure I had eaten well the night before and had a good breakfast. I would bring along two types of Power Bar, two Power Gels or the equivalent, a cup of dried fruit and nuts, and a mouse chunk of cheese. I'd also bring about two liters of water and hydrate really well before starting.

Water Is Life

Drinking after you cramp is futile. Plan on having the right amount of fluid and drink *before* you cramp up. And the right amount? Everyone is different here. There is some minimum to take as far as liters per hour, but you must adjust the quantity of water to bring on a given climb

Peter Coward dying of thirst on Horse Chute. (Greg Murphy)

based on temperature, movement, and availability of water on the route, the approach, and the descent. I take two liters of water for an eight-hour push.

I flavor my water with Champion Nutrition's Revenge. There are electrolytes in sports drinks and other big words that are good for performance. But just as important, your water should taste good so you drink more or more regularly. If you have an ongoing problem with cramping due to hydration problems, check for the potassium and sodium ratios in the drink mix you're using. Often, cheaper drinks do not have much potassium in them—and you may need more of that than plentiful (and cheap) sodium. Consider packing iodine tablets. They are small and light and can render water drinkable that otherwise is not.

Water Bag Versus Water Bottle

The best place to carry water is in your body, but for long hauls you must carry it somewhere else. The hydration systems by companies like Gaia, Platypus, CamelBak, and Ultimate Direction are great inventions. Water bladders are typically carried in small packs with handy little pouches where you can put energy bars, headlamps, etc.

If you wear your water bladder during the ascent, you don't have to "stop" to drink. Frequently the effort to stop and pull a water bottle out of your pack is enough to make you put off drinking, thereby reducing performance. On multipitch routes you are often stopped at a belay waiting for your partner, so this advantage may not be a big deal, as you'll have time to pull out your water bottles. Certainly for soloists, the water bladders have a huge advantage.

Be careful with your water bladder in a chimney. More than once, I've pinched the tube of my water bladder in a chimney and had cold water flowing down my back. This might be refreshing in the Valley during the summer but very uncomfortable in the mountains during a fall ascent. If a water bladder breaks, and they do, you'll lose a lot of valuable water.

Water bottles have their advantages too. They are easier to dip in a stream or collect dribble from the wall. They are simple to clean, which is important if you've used a sports drink. They are easy to hand off between partners. If you are hauling, water bottles are more manageable. They come in a variety of small sizes, like 16 ounces, 32 ounces, etc. Compare this to the 50- and 100-ounce water bladders. I favor using crushable bottles so that you can gain space as the day goes on.

CHAPTER 9
TRAINING

A man who is physically fit performs better at any job. Fatigue makes cowards of us all.
—Vince Lombardi

I (H.F.) could write 50 pages or more on details of specific workouts I've done to peak for competitions or to get ready for adventures like hiking/running the California 14,000-foot peaks, but the following quote of mine stops me: "Knowledge of how to work out is not the difficult part, finding the motivation to do so is the real challenge." I've read about many great training regimes, but they're all useless if you can't keep motivated. Still, I'll mention a few things. . .

The best training for climbing is climbing. If you're comfortable on 5.10, try pushing for speed on a 5.8 or below. You'll learn things on 5.8 routes that you can apply when you're speed climbing 5.6 to 5.12, or A0 to A5. Think about all the tips you've gathered from this book and apply them on a 5.8, not when you're pushing your free climbing limit on 5.12.

French Free

In order to French free quickly, you have to trust that your placements are bomber. The only way to gain this trust is through practice. Aid climbing is a great way to gain confidence in your gear placements. Because every placement is weighted, it is critically evaluated. If it fails, you're going to fall. While developing these skills, make sure to make placements very frequently to minimize the danger of a fall. Realize that cams rotate as you move past them; this does not render them unsafe. Experiment with this—cams often rotate right back into a "load safe" position when the rope pulls down on them, as in a fall.

It is important to remember while French freeing that you are still "free" climbing. Yes, you are using aid and can't claim a free ascent, but view the piece just like a natural hold and continue to use good climbing technique. Make sure you're putting your lead hip to the wall, using drop knees, and driving off good foot placements. Don't get sloppy with your feet just because you're pulling on a cam; that will wear you out in the long run.

Be very conscious of the direction you pull on a piece. Frequently pieces are not omnidirectional. Don't pull up on a stopper in a downward flare. A climber died on the first pitch of Beverley's Tower on the Cookie Cliff in Yosemite by grabbing a placement that was below him. Tragically, this was his only piece and when it pulled he took a fatal ground fall. There are two lessons here. First, never grab your only piece. If you're going to start pulling on gear, make sure you have at least two pieces placed. Second, be very aware of the direction of pull on your placements.

The ability to readily switch from aiding to French freeing to pure free climbing and back to aid climbing is a valuable skill. It's not easy and takes practice, so work on it. Good routes for this are obviously ones that are a bit harder than your free climbing limit. Use aid on the sections that are too hard, use French free techniques for anything within a number grade of your onsight ability, and free the other sections.

Non-climbing Training

It would be hard to think of any activity that would hurt your speed climbing. "That which doesn't kill you, makes you stronger." Swimming is great training. The motion and feel is very similar to speed climbing. If you're hoping to do a one-hour route, go try to swim for an hour in the pool! Shoot, tell me that wouldn't make you strong. I'll point out motivation here again. If it's hard to get psyched for an hour of lap swimming, I'd suggest that you visualize the fun route you're training for while you swim. That way you'll get to enjoy the climb twice.

Lat pull downs are a great climbing exercise. You can use less weight and do a ton more "pull-ups" than you might on a bar. Generally, I (H.F.) try to get in some pushing exercises as well when I'm in the weight room. This helps balance out the pulling muscles, which are constantly exercised while climbing. Climbers have overdeveloped pulling muscles, so seize every chance you get to beef up the pushing muscles. Do bench presses and tricep extensions. Working these pushing exercises in the weight room is a great way to reduce the chances of many overuse injuries in climbing.

Fast Twitch Fibers

Studies have show. . .

1. During a slow powerful movement fast twitch fibers contribute to the motion more so than slow twitch fibers.
2. During a fast powerful movement slow twitch fibers contribute almost zero to the motion.

My (H.F.) conclusion, assuming your performance goal is fast movement, is that when you train motions either with weights or during other activities, you should exaggerate the speed of the motion to recruit fast twitch fibers.

You can't take full advantage of the strength in your legs if your core is not strong enough to transfer that effort to your upper body. Core strength is paramount in all climbing. Work the lower back and those abdominal muscles. Find as many different core exercises as you can—there's plenty. Picture big man John Gill doing his front levers for inspiration or my friend Phil Request, at 6 foot 3 weighing in regularly at 180 pounds, who can hold a front lever for 17.1 seconds. Do stomach crunches, use an ab roller, and do leg raises while you're watching TV. Hang on a bar or door jam and bring your knees to your chest. Lie on your stomach and do the Superman position, lifting your arms and legs up.

If it is available, check out the Versa Climber at the local gym. This is a climbing specific treadmill. You should try climbing on the underside, as well as the topside. Basically you can simulate climbing a 5.4 scramble (on the topside of the machine, normal side), or a 5.10 jug haul (on the bottom side). So basically you can train the climbing movement for a real long time without the need for a belayer! There are a few manufacturers of climbing treadmills out there—Brewer's Ledge is one of them. Find out if there's one at a gym near you.

Skate skiing is also excellent for the speed climbing muscles. You're getting the arms pushing and pulling and the legs working in symphony with the arms. If you use longer poles, you'll get a higher overhead pulling motion.

Mile-High Mileage: A Full Day of Sport Climbing at Colorado's Shelf Road

by Mark Kroese, the author of Fifty Favorite Climbs *and a volunteer member of the Access Fund board of directors*

Nothing fuels my desire to climb like sitting in an all-day meeting—especially when it's with the Access Fund board. Because my fellow directors and I convene just four times per year, our meetings are long and tedious; we author climbing management plans, debate policy issues, approve grants, and review budgets. We talk about climbing, think about climbing, and study the impacts of climbing. We do everything, it seems, except actually go climbing.

After our February meeting, a group of us decided that come hell or high water, we were going to climb. We made plans to spend a day in Eldorado Canyon, just eight miles from the Access Fund offices in Boulder, Colorado. As luck would have it, the weather was perfect on meeting day, but the next morning greeted us with frigid temperatures and swirling snow. The closest warm rock was 150 miles to the south at a limestone crag called Shelf Road.

Undeterred, we piled into Chris Archer's Toyota Forerunner and hung on tight as he blasted down Interstate 25 while sipping a triple tall latte. Our foursome had more in common than our affiliation with the Access Fund. We all climbed at a similar level, and more importantly, we shared the desire to climb lots of pitches. We agreed that this was not a day for "project" climbing; we wanted mileage.

As Becky and Rob planned our itinerary, Chris assured me that each of us would lead ten pitches by the day's end. I reminded him that I had a 9 P.M. flight out of Denver International, which gave us about six hours to climb. "No problem amigo," he said with a confident smile. "We'll be super efficient."

And efficient we were. Before arriving at the crag, Rob reviewed the day's plan. "We'll start on the right side of the Cactus Cliff," he explained, pointing to the guidebook, "and we'll work left. This way, we'll do the harder routes first, and follow the path of the sun." Rob also suggested that we save hiking time by climbing at only one of

Shelf's many cliffs. We nodded in agreement, and as if breaking from a huddle, jumped out of the car and got to work.

Rob and Becky took the first leads, climbing 20 feet apart on neighboring routes. Within ten minutes both had clipped into the chains and were being lowered to the ground. As soon as Rob untied from the rope, I pulled it into the rope bag and he loosened his shoes. (We all chose to lead every route). I was on belay within 60 seconds and began pocket pulling my way to the anchors, clipping Rob's pre-placed quick draws as I went. Instead of threading the rope through the chains and unclipping the quick draws as Rob lowered me to the ground, I left the route equipped.

Sticking to our plan, we simply swapped routes with Chris and Becky. This way, only the first climber would need to place the quick draws, and only the fourth would have to floss the chains and remove them. The second and third climbers could simply clip, go, and lower. Our plan worked like a charm. After the first hour of climbing we'd each done three leads—a total of twelve pitches for the group.

We worked our way down the cliff with assembly-line efficiency, breaking for lunch after we'd done six climbs apiece. Because the last four routes were easier than the first six, we decided to climb in "blocks." Rather than follow a pattern of leading, belaying, then leading again, we would each lead two pitches in a row, and then belay twice in a row. This technique saves on transition time and builds endurance. After getting lowered to the ground, the leader stays tied into the rope (and in his shoes). The belayer pulls the rope through the anchors while the leader walks to the base of the next climb and scopes out the initial moves. Assuming adjacent routes, the leader spends less than a minute on the ground in between climbs.

Five hours after arriving at the base of the Cactus Cliff, we each completed our tenth route of the day. We all had wooden forearms, sore feet, and trashed fingertips, but the satisfaction of logging a thousand feet of limestone sport climbing made it all worthwhile. It was the perfect way to start the season. On the way home, Chris guzzled another triple latte, while the rest of us demonstrated how efficiently we could sleep.

Cardiovascular Training

The fastest climbers on long routes all possess great cardiovascular fitness. Your workout should involve a lot of climbing, that's what we love to do, right? I (B.W.) like climbing in any form: running up a ridge, hiking a steep approach, biking uphill, etc. Running is one of the best ways to improve your cardio fitness, and trail running is the most fun. It requires greater agility than road running because of the varied terrain, and the varied movement helps prevent repetitive stress injuries. The softer surface of the trails further reduces injury potential. Swimming and cross-country skiing are also great climbing exercises.

Running, skiing, and biking have all been used to enchain routes. If this is your game, then all the more reason to train your cardiovascular system. When Roger Briggs trained to break the record on the Longs Peak Triathlon—a human powered trilogy that involved biking from Boulder to the trailhead (38 miles, 3,600 vertical feet), running to the base of the face (4 miles, 3,000 vertical feet), and climbing the Diamond (11 pitches, 5.10a/b)—he didn't train his climbing speed at all. He just worked on biking and trail running.

Motivation

"It is not enough to have the will to win. You have to have the will to prepare to win!" I (B.W.) forget who said it, but there are no truer words. When Santiago Botero was caught and passed by Lance Armstrong on a savage climb during the 2000 Tour de France, Santiago knew that he had lost the race months before it started. Armstrong's smile said to him, "I was training while you were sleeping, Santiago. I won this race months ago when you were selecting which bike to ride. I was punishing myself in these mountains. I was preparing myself to win." To perform at your peak, you'll need to train. And training is hard.

The key is to find the motivation. It's great, and ideal, to work on your weaknesses, but if you can only get motivated to do what you're already good at, at least you're working out. Have fun—make it fun! Bill and I both wear MP3 players while running, climbing, and hiking solo. Put together a collection of inspirational music and visualize yourself smoking up a route in record time. Visualize, visualize, visualize! Think of cruising the Nose in six hours on a 70-degree day in June and casually getting back to the Valley floor and going for an ice cream by late afternoon! (This is what I do. Bill dreams of getting down in time for breakfast.)

CHAPTER 10
COMPETITIONS AND SPORT ROUTES

I love climbing precisely because it's pure play. Sure sponsorships and sport climbing competitions have changed the equation (i.e. people are starting to train), but for things like big wall speed climbing, it's still a bunch of friendly yahoos in pursuit of a worthless goal. It's nothing but fun. And thus most of the speed records are "soft." I'm sure with some training there's another [half hour to an hour] of slop to be shaved off both the Salathé and Half Dome records.

—Jim Herson, holder of both the Salathé
and Half Dome speed records

Imagine clawing your way up a gently overhanging 60-foot wall as fast as you can on holds about the size of baseballs. A rival climber, usually only a body length to your side, is trying to claw faster than you on an identical route. To top it off there's an announcer blaring over the microphone and a thousand Gen-Xer's screaming at you. It's similar to the crazy scene on the TV show *American Gladiators* only Goliath isn't chasing you. Ah, the X-Games experience!

What do you do with wacky sports that don't quite make it into the Olympics? You make your own wacky Olympics—the X-Games—which is basically a collection of wild sports that don't fit the Greek idea of an Olympic sport. Skateboarding, skysurfing, motocross, street luge—and now climbing. Of the climbing events, speed climbing was the most popular with the TV crowd, so much so that it is now the only climbing event in the X-Games.

There is not a standard wall for speed climbing competitions, and routes can be rated from 5.6 to 5.12 depending on the level of the competition and the organizer's particular goals. Speed climbers usually com-

St. Polten, Austria, World Cup 1992. (Hans Florine)

pete well below their top level. The route for the X-Games is rated 5.9+, and the fastest time in 2000 was 11.54 seconds! The more experienced speed climbers make it look like swimming or sprinting rather than climbing. I (H.F.) usually set the speed route for local competitions at 5.5 so that four-foot kids and six-foot adults can compete on the same route. Sometimes the winning time is under five seconds.

Training for Competitions

As with any other endeavor, sport specific training is the key to speed climbing. If you want to be a fast climber, practice climbing fast! After you warm up on some very easy routes, pick a route that you're comfortable on and climb up it at a faster than "normal" pace. In general you should speed climb at a grade or two below your hardest ability. Look at the route again when you finish. Check out where you might skip holds or sequence your hands better to avoid extra movements that don't add to upward progress, like a drop knee. Often your butt is out from the wall quite a bit when you speed climb because you are driving your feet at a 45-degree angle to the wall. This makes your feet stick even if you don't hit a foothold.

Tips for Competition

1. Practice on a route several grades below your limit first.

2. Try *not* to look at your feet. Think of your feet as having a memory of where your hands just were.

3. Use imagery. Images are always good for learning technique. For instance, imagine swimming up the route or throwing the holds to the ground.

4. Generally, two short moves are faster than a strained long move.

5. If a competition allows, study how the other competitors are speeding up the route.

6. Try to drive off big holds with your legs. Think of pushing off the wall with your feet at a 45-degree angle rather than pushing straight down. This makes your feet stick even if you miss a hold.

7. If you're competing and you can rehearse a route, practice the last 15 feet of the route more than any other part. Figure out the lowest point from which you can dyno for the bell.

8. Never, never give up! The other competitors may slip or fumble too. Go hard until you hit the bell.

Try to envision "throwing the holds to the ground" or "swimming up the route" without definitive stops and starts. If you can't move fluidly through the route, then get on something less difficult. Rest for two to six minutes and give it another go using the sequence you think is fastest. One sequence of holds will not be the fastest for every competitor. Find the sequence that works best for you. At most competitions you'll need to have the stamina to climb fast for four to ten races with 1- to 15-minute rests in between. If you can, find out the format for the event and mimic it in your training.

If you have aspirations of competing in the X-Games, you'll want to find a 60-foot wall. It is unlikely that you have one at your disposal, and few climbing gyms are over 40 feet tall, let alone 60. Still, a gym is a great place to start regardless of the height. Climb a 5.9 jug haul on the longest wall you can find. Try different hand and foot sequences. Have someone start you off the ground with starting commands: "Ready, Set, Go!" For more

Tips for Sport Routes

Many folks can run to a local sport crag or climbing gym after work; and when you only have a short amount of time to get your climbing in, it can be important to climb efficiently. Here are some tips.

1. Whether all climbers are leading or one or more following, do not thread through the anchors until the last person in your party climbs. This has you belaying off the quick draws until the last person lowers, which protects the fixed gear from excess wear and eliminates all but the last person doing the thread operation. This should be the process regardless of the fixed gear: chains, carabiners, cold shuts, rap rings, etc.

2. When the anchors are two chains, do not clip into the bottom links because that is where you'll need to thread the rope after the last person in your party climbs.

3. Having a "cow's tail" or daisy chain on your harness can speed up your changeover at the anchor when you thread the rope. Quick draws from the route you just cleaned work also.

4. Thread rope *behind* the draws or daisy that you are hanging on so that when you are weighting the rope for the lowering there is no tension on the biners for removal.

5. Think out the best sequence of climbers in your group to keep people climbing. For example, if you have three people, a simple rotation has each person climbing, belaying, and resting (which includes tying shoes on and getting ready to climb). Then repeat. In other words, when the climber hits the ground, the person resting has his shoes on and is ready to tie into the rope for the next ascent. The belayer now becomes the person getting ready, and the climber goes to belay duty.

6. When someone who is not in your party is about to climb a route that you want to get on, offer use of your draws to them. When they are finished they can simply lower off, pull their rope, and waste none of your time going through the threading and cleaning process.

information on the X-Games, log on to www.expn.go.com.

If the competition allows, study how other competitors are speeding up the route. Focus on competitors who have the same body type, strengths, and weaknesses that you do. Take the best beta for each section from all the competitors and make a winning hybrid beta for yourself.

Here are some drills to practice. Try climbing a route fast and not looking below your chest. This forces you to remember where the holds are for your feet. The idea is not to stall your upward momentum by looking down. Next try double-hand dynos up the route. For some sections of a climb, it may be faster to double dyno. Set up for the dyno by dropping low and hiking your feet high. Launch for the next hold and repeat rather than trying to climb smoothly through the section. And, practicing for pure speed is a great way to improve your climbing reflexes. Hold a friendly competition between some climbers at the gym.

Non-climbing Training

Because getting time in a gym isn't always convenient, include some cross-training activities in your workout like swimming, rowing, and weightlifting. When I swim I try to freestyle sprint one length of the pool—which takes approximately the same time as it would to run up the speed wall at the X-Games. Once you get strong, try this drill with swimmer's paddles so that your arms get more resistance. Finally, substitute leg thrusts for your flutter kick. Bring your knees up to your waist as if you were mimicking the leg drive of pushing off a hold on the climbing wall. This motion looks ridiculous—like you're trying to dog paddle really fast and failing miserably—but it is effective training.

If you're lucky enough to actually get into a scull and row, that's keen; but if all you have is a rowing machine at your local health club, that will work also. Always warm up, then try doing sprints at 80-, 90-, and 100-percent effort for 10 to 30 seconds. Again, match the time it would take to go up a speed route. Rest for two to eight minutes in between sprints.

In the weight room, I try to mimic the sweeping motion your arm makes when you are climbing fast on the lat pull down machine or similar device. This is good for keeping your arm speed up. Use light enough weight so that you can pull down as fast or faster than you would when speed climbing. Be careful when you do this because it's easy to slam the weights into the top of the weight machine.

The Principle of Applying Speed on Short Routes
by Hans Florine

Thirteen years ago I had climbed only one 5.12. With my head held high, I went climbing at Stony Point in Southern California. After warming up, I put a toprope on a 5.12 route. On this testpiece, I ended up hanging on the route twice for my first burn. After quite a struggle, I got to the top. This took me about 10 or 15 minutes.

From around the rock, my friend Andres Puhvel reared his large bulbous head with a gleaming grin on his face. Andres had recently beat me in a difficulty competition (by a hair) and had lost to me in a speed competition. Andres climbed at the same level as I did at the time. Maybe he had done one other 5.12. We had a friendly rivalry.

"Looks like a nice route," Andres said, "Do you mind if I try?" Reluctantly, I let him borrow the toprope on the route. He climbed it with no falls on his first try in about four or five minutes. "You looked very smooth," I said gnashing my teeth. "It's really pretty simple," he said. Then he admitted to having done the route before. My jaw relaxed. He had done the route before so he had the beta.

"Hey Hans," said Andres with the smile on his face widening, "Let's see who can get up it faster." "Not interested," I said. "I haven't even climbed it yet. I can't even climb it slowly." I roped up for my second attempt and made it without falling. I didn't time it, but I'd guess it took about four minutes. Andres got on the route again and asked us to time him. He climbed the route in 2 minutes and 20 seconds! Then he proceeded to dare me to beat that.

I'm not one to back down on a dare, especially if it involves food or climbing, so I agreed. I didn't know whether I'd even make it without hanging on the rope. When the dust had settled, I'd climbed the route in 1 minute and 50 seconds!

Naturally, Andres could not let things stand and had to give it another go. He did it in 1 minute 20 seconds. On my next try, I did it in 58 seconds! Andres went again and did it in 52 seconds! I thought, "Here's a route I couldn't even do three hours ago and now I'm racing up it in 58 seconds." It took me far less energy to do it in 58 seconds than when I'd hung on it for ten minutes.

This experience brilliantly illustrated to me the importance of speed on short routes. Here's the moral of the story, kids. What I was doing the first time was doubting my way up the route. Later, I moved with decisiveness and confidence, and went through each move easily. To me, this was a significant revelation. Applying this observation to climbing made me start onsight climbing at a little faster pace. My onsight level went from 5.11d to 5.12c inside of ten months! I thought, "There's gotta be something to this speed thing."

My friendly rivalry with Andres did not end that day at Stoney Point. Andres called me a week later and said he'd climbed the route in 38 seconds! I grabbed my gear and got in the car.

Speed on Sport Routes

Many climbers scoff at the mention of speed climbing as an esoteric pursuit practiced by a small minority of either competition climbers or big wall speed demons. But methods from speed climbing and massive enchainments have been applied to short, one-pitch routes as well. In Joshua Tree National Monument, in the Yosemite off-season, John Bacher was infamous for soloing a "Half Dome Day" or an "El Cap Day." This involved linking together 20 to 30 routes in a single day so that the total vertical feet climbed equaled Half Dome or El Cap.

Linking routes together is quite natural for climbers with big appetites and only small local rocks. Just as the French started their enchainments of big alpine routes in order to simulate bigger mountains, the small crag climber can enchain many routes to simulate a much bigger cliff. Speed and endurance have also been applied to bouldering problems. An Internet Web site called Birthday Challenge (www.birthdaychallenge. om) describes participants stringing together hundreds of bouldering problems in a single marathon day.

While speed is obviously necessary in order to climb as much as possible in a given time period, it can also be a key to successfully climbing difficult routes. A conscious attempt to speed climb may help you succeed on routes you've failed on before. How can you speed climb a route that you can't even climb at a relaxed pace? Speed can actually help you climb more efficiently by reducing technique hindering inhibition and pessimism, which in turn lets your body do what it should be doing automatically and unconsciously.

CHAPTER 11
ETHICS AND STYLE

Badges? Badges? We don't need no stinkin' badges!

—Paraphrased from the movie *Treasure of the Sierra Madre*

Rules for speed climbing? Rules?! Why not? We have specific rules for what constitutes a redpoint (though sport climbers have changed the rules on what constitutes a redpoint over the last ten years). Why not specific rules for speed climbing ascents? To have a "record" for a route, certain standards must be followed. At the very least we need to ensure that the competitors are playing by the same rules.

Fixed lines

In Yosemite, a set of informal rules has traditionally been used. While clipping fixed gear is allowed, using pre-placed fixed ropes is not. Obviously, pre-fixing ropes will make the next day's ascent go faster, and lots of non-speed teams use this approach. It is common to fix ropes down from Sickle Ledge on the Nose and down from Heart Ledges on the Salathé. But on a speed ascent, the official start time is when the team first leaves the ground.

If the first time the team leaves the ground they are fixing lines and plan to return tomorrow, then the fixing day is the start time. This seems logical. Otherwise all speed records would degenerate into speed jugging contests up fixed lines. It might be speedy, speedy jugging, but it's not speedy climbing. Spelunkers Chuck Henson (50-years-young) and Pat Smith both had a time of 1 hour and 12 minutes up El Cap on a fixed line strung right next to the Nose. So the record that Peter Croft and I (H.F.) set of 4 hours and 22 minutes isn't *really* the fastest ascent of the Nose.

The ban on fixed lines isn't a new rule for Yosemite speed climbing. It was first established back in the Golden Age of Yosemite. An early reference to this ethic appears in Steve Roper's *Camp 4*. He recounts the first one-day ascent of the Northwest Face of Half Dome in 1966. He had "no thought whatsoever of fixing pitches the night before—that would have been cheating." Not only was this the first one-day ascent of Half Dome but also the first one-day ascent of a grade VI climb. Another grade VI climb would not be completed in a day until the Nose was done nine years later. It seems obvious that using someone else's fixed lines is also a violation.

A controversy arose over the fixed rope issue and consideration when passing other parties when Miles Smart reported his record solo of 9 hours and 15 minutes for the Zodiac. (The Zodiac is a very overhanging aid route on the southeast face of El Capitan.) This came just a week after Russ Mitrovich shocked the world by soloing this route without a rope in 12 hours—the first time an aid route of such length was done without a rope (see *Climbing* 190). The debate revolved around the fact that Miles Smart used another party's fixed lines to protect himself (he didn't weight the lines) and took a belay while passing a party (see *Climbing* 194). Smart originally didn't report these details and hence the uproar. As reported in *Climbing* 195, he claimed that using these techniques was "simple courtesy and sound mountaineering judgment" that allowed him "to pass them [the other party] quickly and efficiently, and avoid making them wait [while he led, rappelled, and cleaned to pass them]."

While this is true, and the other party probably appreciated his kindness, it does invalidate the record. Says who? Well, the climbing community in general. Most climbers consider Russ Mitrovich's ascent as the solo record on the Zodiac. Could Miles have gone faster and gotten the record on the route if the parties weren't there? Maybe.

In the alpine world, using established fixed ropes is usually considered fair game. When Reinhold Messner and Peter Habeler climbed the Eiger North Face in a then record ten hours, they used fixed lines that had been strung on the Difficult Crack by the Eiger Sanction film crew. The team freely admitted to using the ropes and didn't claim any speed record—though it was the fastest the face had been climbed to date. Alpine climbing is different than blitzing up the walls of Yosemite. In alpine climbing you do what's necessary to keep yourself alive.

Hans on second variation Pitch of Beggars Buttress 5.11. (Mark Kroese)

Timing a Technical Rock Climb

1. Start the stopwatch when the first person in your party starts climbing where a "normal party" would start climbing.
2. Stop the time when the last person in your party and all the gear you're walking down with reaches the top where a "normal party" would walk off.

Are there exceptions to this rule? Of course! I like to use a "car-to-car" time. This is easy enough to figure out. (Car-to-car times get complicated if you drive between enchained routes.) Bill, on the other hand, prefers a more specific starting location in order to eliminate the advantage of a good parking spot. For instance, the Half Dome Run starts at the sign indicating it is 8.2 miles to the summit.

Start and finish times

Is a committee required to certify speed records? Smart says, ". . . until Yosemite appoints its own version of the International Olympic Committee (IOC) to impose rules. . . the only fact that will never be disputable is the time you started on the Valley floor and the time you finished on El Cap's rim." Actually, that isn't true. In 1966 when Jim Madsen and Kim Schmitz were setting new standards for speed in Yosemite Valley, speed ascents were less rigorously timed. Instead of using hours and minutes, days and half days were used. As noted in Roper's book *Camp 4*, a somewhat jealous Royal Robbins stated, "Some climbers are extremely liberal in their interpretation of a 'halfday.' It has a tendency to run up to 5 or 6 P.M." Like Smart, some of the Madsen/Schmitz speed ascents were also tainted by the use of fixed lines.

Leaver biners

What about "leaver biners?" Normally the rule is that all gear must be hauled to the top before the clock stops, and the implication is that gear will not be left behind regardless. However, leaver biners seem to be an accepted speed strategy, but let's take it to absurd levels for the sake of an argument. What if a rich solo speed climber raced up a route with a couple of spare ropes and an unbelievable amount of gear, then left it all behind? This ridiculous example illustrates the difficulty in drawing the line between what is allowed and what is not.

Cache of sorts

Another "style issue" involves stashing water, food, or gear along a route, or in between routes before you've started a single push ascent. Heck, Mark Overson once stashed a partner! He was doing a long traverse with one section that required a rope and a belay. He met his partner in the middle of the traverse, and picked up gear, food, water, and a climbing partner. Once the technical section was complete, he continued the traverse solo. Doing a "violation" like this is not grounds for excommunication from the climbing community; it's just important that you divulge the style in which you did the ascent. Why? Because if someone wants to "repeat da feat," they'll know how to plan their adventure.

Bottom line

The bottom line is that almost no one cares about speed climbing, except the speed climbers. I'll be the first to say that climbing is silly. To make rules about it is just piling ridiculous on top of silly. My biggest rule, if I were the "rule maker," would be that climbers be honest about what they did. Then it is up to the climbing community to credit them with the glory, if any. The "rule maker" thought of something else. You should be having fun. If you're not having fun, then make you're own rules so that you are. If outright lying or intentionally hiding "crucial details" about an ascent is fun for you, then I have no platform to talk to you, and personally, I'm not interested in your adventures.

I'm a firm believer that the power of competition drives humans to better their achievements. Competition is *healthy*! It is competition that has pushed the world's greatest athletes to achieve heights previously unimagined. If we don't try to standardize how we're timing ourselves on routes, we can't compare our efforts. If we can't compare our efforts, we can't see if we're improving. The Brits call it "burning off your mates." The idea is to build on your mates' achievements. Hopefully this attitude is reciprocal and we'll motivate them to get off the sofa and go best our effort. This continual supportive and competitive atmosphere improves everyone.

CHAPTER 12
THE HISTORY OF SPEED CLIMBING

Few places in the world are more dangerous than home. Fear not, therefore, to try the mountain-passes. They will eliminate care, save you from deadly apathy, set you free, and call forth every faculty into vigorous, enthusiastic action.
—John Muir (1894)

For most of its illustrious history, climbing has been celebrated as a "non-competitive" sport. When the first speed climbing contests were taking place in Eastern Europe, most of the climbing world frowned on such overt competition. Climbing, they thought, wasn't about speed; it was about ethics, difficulty, purity of line, and spirit. But climbing can be about speed, and there has always been competition in the climbing world. In some ways, it's just like running, biking, and skiing—no sooner were these sports being practiced than they were measured by the clock. Like it or not, a climber's skill is often measured by how fast he does a route.

By most accounts, modern climbing started with Balmat and Paccard's ascent of Mt. Blanc in 1786. Climbing has since expanded from pure alpine into every modern facet of ascension; and speed has been introduced into each facet. In 1950, a client bet Hermann Buhl that he couldn't ascend and descend the Biancograt (north ridge) of the Piz Bernina from the Boval Hut in under six hours. The climb involved 1,000 meters of climbing, and Buhl made it with not a minute to spare. Supposedly he descended 500 meters of steep snow on the very exposed ridge in only 15 minutes.

The North Face of the Eiger

The North Face of the Eiger is one of the most infamous objectives in the climbing world, known prior to World War II as the "last great problem." Nine climbers died trying to climb this face before it was successfully climbed in 1938. All of those who died were caught in bad weather, a major contributor to their deaths.

The Eiger rarely has good weather for many days in a row. In 1998 there was supposed to be a live TV ascent of the Eigerwand. The whole crew waited for good weather for 45 days, and the ascent didn't occur until the next year. If you could climb the face in a single day, your chances of getting good weather would greatly improve.

On August 14, 1974, when Reinhold Messner and Peter Habeler climbed the North Face of the Eiger in a record ten hours—in 1950, it was first done in a day—Messner wrote about the fast ascent: "I didn't climb the Eiger in 10 hours to set up any new record but in order to eliminate a large proportion of the danger."

In 1983, Thomas Bubendorfer of Austria set the still-standing record of 4 hours and 50 minutes.

Yosemite

While speed climbing is practiced somewhat differently throughout many sub-disciplines, it has been most visible in big wall climbing. When it comes to climbing big walls, there is no better place in the world than Yosemite—especially to push the limits of speed. The relatively benign climate and ease of rescue make Yosemite an ideal place to stick your neck out. I must hasten to add that I know of no speed climbing team that has been rescued from the walls of Yosemite, but certainly some unpleasant and unplanned bivys have occurred for overly ambitious climbers.

When speed first came to the big walls of Yosemite it was more because of style than anything else. Royal Robbins was the standard bearer for the Valley. He was interested in bold, hard first ascents that pushed up the standards. Robbins didn't think much about speed, but he didn't ignore it either, because he knew it was a measure of competency. His second ascent of the Nose, with Tom Frost, Chuck Pratt, and Joe Fitschen, cut the time down from 18 months to 7 days. Of course, it is unfair to compare a second ascent to the first ascent because the first leaders had to place a number of bolts, and more so, had to overcome the psychological challenges of wondering if the route was possible.

Warren Harding on the Nose in 1956, prior to the first ascent. (Allen Steck)

Afterwards Robbins predicted, "The day will probably come when this climb [the Nose] will be done in five days, perhaps less." Robbins could hardly foresee that the Nose would someday be climbed in less than five hours!

When Steve Roper and Frank Sacherer ran up Steck-Salathé on Sentinel Rock in only eight and a half hours, Robbins immediately responded. Robbins and Fitschen had been the first party to climb the route in a day (and the only party up to the time of Roper's ascent). Robbins waited an entire day before heading up to Sentinel with Frost. For the first time simul-climbing techniques were used on a big wall in Yosemite. They did the route in 3 hours and 15 minutes! But in general Robbins wasn't drawn to setting speed records; it was Roper who was attracted to such challenges.

Roper was one of the first Yosemite speed climbers. He was motivated by a desire to haul less and gain the respect of his peers. It simplified things if you could climb fast, because in the 1960s hauling was back-breaking work. Roper noticed that routes done over two days involved only 15 to 20 hours of climbing. He figured you could "start early and climb a little faster, take less shit, and do it in 12 (hours)."

One-upmanship also began to play a bigger role, and route times were kept more meticulously. Roper confided, "A question asked more and more this year (1961) was 'How long did you take?' I was guilty of this, trying hard to make my mark doing what I was good at."

Back then climbers didn't pursue records overtly, but anyone finishing a fearsome route in good style, which generally meant getting back down before the bar closed, was highly respected.

Roper was a naturally fast free climber and a very efficient aid climber. He became the first person to climb the classic 17-pitch Royal Arches route (5.7, A0) in Yosemite Valley in under an hour—foreshadowing the current trend of car-to-car speed ascents of this route. His most significant achievement in speed climbing was the first one-day ascent of the Northwest Face on Half Dome in 1966 with Jeff Foott—a feat rarely equaled today. Roper recalls the ascent. "Sixteen long, long tiring hours, me starting the first pitch with hand clutching the first hold, waiting for it to get light enough to leap upward. No such thing as headlamps in those days. And no thought whatsoever of fixing pitches the night before—that would have been cheating."

In an article for the 1972 *American Alpine Journal*, Peter Haan wrote about his first solo of the Salathé Wall. He mused ". . . all this damned hauling. If only one could just climb—climb without bags, water, packs, shoes, rurps, ropes, porters, maps, oxygen, and radios—merely as an incandescent unfettered being given to ascension, upwardness, climbing would not have the trembling impact it has."

The Nose

By 1974, El Capitan had already been climbed in a day, but by the much easier and shorter West Face route. The Nose was the big prize and the desire to climb this route in a single day led to speed climbing's biggest impact on the general climbing world.

In the spring of 1974, Ray Jardine traveled to Yosemite with Lou Dawson and Kris Walker and the world's only supply of a radical new devices called Friends. His goal was to climb the Nose in a single day. He first fixed ropes to Sickle Ledge and then tried for the top the next day. They got pinned down by a storm around the Great Roof and were forced to bivy, but they had completed the first one-bivy ascent of the Nose. The first one-day ascent wouldn't occur until the next year. Jim Bridwell wanted to make a statement about the superiority of American rock climbers and to this end he recruited John Long and Billy Westbay. In line with their patriotic feelings, they planned the ascent for Memorial Day of the next year.

Bridwell's team easily climbed the Nose in a day, taking only 15 hours. While this was only the second time a grade VI climb had been done in a day, the ascent was a breakthrough for a number of other reasons. The route was broken into just three blocks and one climber led everything in that block before turning the lead over to the next climber. The climb also employed the three-man caterpillar technique to keep the leader moving as much as possible. This three-man technique would be the dominant speed-climbing strategy for the next twenty years. Steve Gerbadine, Scott Stowe, and Dave Bengsten would use this technique to do many single push ascents and bag the first one-day ascents of many of Yosemite's grade VIs.

Getting in More Climbing!

With the doors now open, speed-climbing feats occurred regularly in the Valley and the evolution continued through the first solo of El Capitan and the first solo of the Nose. With solo ascents of the biggest routes being done in a day, the next step was obvious: multiple routes in a day.

The most notable was John Bachar's and Peter Croft's 1986 climb of the Nose on El Capitan and the RNWF on Half Dome in a day. In 1998 Hans and Steve Schneider became the first and only people to climb three El Cap routes in a single day. They did the Nose, Lurking Fear, and the West Face in 23 hours and 30 minutes. Croft and Dave Schultz are still the only ones to climb the Nose and the Salathé in a day. In June 2001 Jim Herson and Peter Coward climbed the Salathé and the Regular Northwest Face on Half Dome in 23 hours.

The next step up was to link the big walls via solos. Dean Potter was the first one to do El Cap and Half Dome solo in a single day in 1999. With Potter's feat unbeknownst to him, Hans Florine links the same two routes, in reverse order, also in a day. The next year Florine was the first to solo two El Cap routes in a day when he soloed Lurking Fear and the West Face of El Cap, setting solo records on both.

In 2000 Potter and Timmy O'Neill upped the ante once again. They started with simul-climbing the Regular Northwest Face on Half Dome, then descended the slabs down to the Valley floor and biked (a completely human-powered day) over to the Four Mile Trailhead. In an almost unbelievable time of two and a half hours, they approached, simul-soloed (no rope), and descended from the Steck-Salathé on Sentinel Rock—17 pitches of fearsome chimney climbing with a 5.10b crux section. After more food and another short bike ride, they climbed the Nose on El Cap, finishing at 23 hours and change after starting up Half Dome.

The Current State of the Art

The start of the 1990s marked the pervasive use of hard free climbing and simul-climbing as a means to speed. The three-person caterpillar style was still the favored speed method until about the mid-90s. In 1994, Rolando Garibotti started making prevalent use of "short-fixing." This technique provided for almost continual upward motion of a two-man team. Garibotti preferred this method because it was "so hard to find three partners willing to give 100 percent."

Garibotti, who'd later best Alex Lowe's time on the Grand Traverse, was not only very fast, but also very fit. He set records on a host of walls including Lurking Fear and the Shield using this short-fixing technique. This method was so successful that it has almost completely taken over the speed-climbing scene.

In the late 1990s another speed climbing trend started, and this time it was extremely competitive. No longer could simply moving efficiently and being experienced on the route obtain a record. The major players in this game were among the fastest in the world, and everyone knew the tricks. Simul-climbing and short-fixing became much more prevalent. In the speed soloing game, new tools such as the Silent Partner were coupled with bold soloing and "leaver biners" to set unprecedented times on the big walls.

Finally, the technique of soloing aid without the use of a rope has been used as of late. The boldest example of this technique was Russ Mitrovitch's 1999 12-hour solo of the Zodiac. Mitrovich climbed the entire route sans rope (except for one ten foot section) by using a system of three daisy chains such that he is always clipped into at least two pieces of gear.

The Future

As we go to press, I've just learned that in June 2001 Steve House and Rolando Garibotti climbed Alaska's Infinite Spur, a 9,000-foot sweep of granite and ice, in a blistering fast 25 hours. The test piece line on the south face of Mt. Foraker had seen only three repeats since its first ascent in 1977, and the fastest previous climb was seven days. House and Garibotti climbed with small packs and a single rope, and they simul-climbed most of the route. The jumps in speed, enchainments, unroped climbing, and 5.13 free climbing that characterized speed climbing developments in 1999 and 2000 were amazing. In the short term it will be more of the same, with route times getting faster and faster.

Speed climbing has at times been pursued very competitively and at times out of necessity, but perhaps it occurs most often just for pure fun. When Chris McNamara topped out after shattering the record on the Shield with Cedar Wright, he felt "one of the most incredible highs of my life." Duane Raleigh has written, "Once you get the taste for it [speed climbing] . . . you're ruined. . . . Speed gets your juices pumping." The ability to move quickly by cutting out extraneous gear provides a joyous sensation of unrestricted motion. Nowhere is this more exemplified than in Canadian Guy Edwards' 19-minute roundtrip solo of the classic West Ridge of Pigeon Spire, where he stripped weight to the absolute minimum:

"I've soloed the West Ridge before, but I thought in order to achieve a sub-20 minute time, I needed to go as light as possible. Soloing is about freedom; and soloing naked is a very liberating experience, kind of like skinny dipping. . . total ecstasy!"

Highlights and Speed Records

Speed breakthroughs are the big news in climbing, and following are the highlights of the past half-century.

1950: First one-day ascent of the Eiger North Face. Erich Waschak and Leo Forstenlechner climbed the 1938 Heckmair route in 18 hours.

July 1959: John Day and Jim and Lou Whittaker climb Rainier round trip from Paradise (elevation gain about 9,000 feet) in 7:20 and spark an early competition for speed. Two weeks later guides Dick McGowan and Gil Blinn make the trip in 6:40.

Summer 1961: Steve Roper reads Hermann Buhl and is prompted to make a mostly **unroped solo** of the Royal Arches route (5.7, A0) in under an hour. This same style of mostly unroped soloing would be applied by Dean Potter 37 years later on the Regular Northwest Face of Half Dome (5.11d, A0).

1961: Claudio Barbier links up all five north faces of the Tre Cime di Lavaredo in the Dolomites in a single day–one of the first big **enchainments**. This is the vertical equivalent of El Capitan and Half Dome.

September 1961: Steve Roper and Frank Sacherer onsight the Steck-Salathé in 8:30. This is the first one-day onsight of a grade V route.

September 1961: Royal Robbins and Tom Frost climb the Steck-Salathé in 3:15, introduce **simul-climbing** techniques and **overtly competitive** speed climbing to the Valley.

July 13, 1963: Layton Kor and Royal Robbins make the first one-day ascent of the Diamond on Longs Peak.

Summer 1964: Federick Morshead climbs Mt. Blanc from Chamonix in a roundtrip time of 16.5 hours.

May 1966: Steve Roper and Jeff Foot climb the Regular Northwest Face of Half Dome in a day. This is the first one-day ascent of a grade VI route. They establish the rule of **no fixed lines** for a one-day ascent.

July 19, 1969: Reinhold Messner solos the North Face of Les Droites, the route's first one-day ascent.

Spring 1974: Ray Jardine, along with Lou Dawson and Kris Walker, climb the Nose of El Cap in 28 hours spread over three days. Their extraordinary speed was partially due to using the world's only supply of **Friends**. Jardine had "invented Friends specifically with a speed climb of the Nose in mind."

1974: The "Climbing Smiths" (father George Smith and sons Flint, Quade, Cody, and Tyle) climbed all 54 Colorado 14ers in 33 days and then continued on to California and Washington to climb all 68 (nowadays 15 mountains in California are considered 14ers) mountains over 14,000 feet in the lower 48 states in a still standing record of 48 days.

August 14, 1974: Reinhold Messner and Peter Habeler onsight the North Face of the Eiger in a record 10 hours. News of this ascent inspires Jim Bridwell to respond with an American version of speed climbing. A year later he climbs the Nose in a day.

June 21, 1975: John Long, Billy Westbay, and Jim Bridwell make the first one-day ascent of the Nose. They easily climb it in a day and take only 15 hours to cover the route. This is now the canonical speed-climbing goal—Nose in a day (NIAD).

1975: Reinhold Messner and Peter Habeler make the first alpine style ascent of an 8000-meter peak when they climb Hidden Peak, cutting the ascent time for 8000-meter peaks from months down to days.

June 1978: Galen Rowell and Ned Gillette, a former Olympic cross-country skier, climb Mt. McKinley in a single day.

1980: Reinhold Messner solos the North Face of Everest in just 3 days. It is the first time Everest had ever been soloed and by far the fastest ascent.

July 14, 1980: Steve Monks (UK) onsight solos the first ascent of the Casual Route on the Diamond (four years before the normally credited first solo by Charlie Fowler), all free, in under three hours.

September 27, 1980: Steve Monks solos the Regular Northwest Face of Half Dome in under seven hours, using a rope only on pitch 4, the Robbin's Traverse, and above Big Sandy Ledges. The style is quite similar to that used by Dean Potter on the same route 18 years later, but the ascent isn't publicized and doesn't have an impact on Valley speed climbing.

May 25–28, 1982: Alex MacIntyre, Roger Baxter-Jones, and Doug Scott flash the first ascent of Shishapangma's (8046m) South Face. They climb the 2500-meter face in four days.

June 1982: Christophe Profit free solos the American Direct Route on the Dru in 3:10. He uses a helicopter to approach the route and then is supplied with mixed climbing gear on the summit but is very open about his style. The route is 3,000 feet high and involves climbing up to 5.11.

Summer 1982: Jim Beyer solos the West Face of El Cap in 23:30. It is the first time El Cap is soloed in a day.

1983: Thomas Budendorfer sets the still standing solo record of 4.5 hours on the Eiger North Face.

1984: Reinhold Messner and Hans Kammerlander are the first to link-up 8000-meter peaks when they traverse Gasherbrum I and II in four days.

1984: Krzysztof Wielicki makes the first one-day ascent of an 8000-meter peak when he climbs from base camp to the summit of Broad Peak in 17 hours. However this was not a completely solo ascent and the route had been at least partially prepared.

Summer 1985: Christophe Profit climbs the North Faces of the Eiger (6:45), the Matterhorn (4 hours), and the Grandes Jorasses via the Linceul, aka the Shroud, (4 hours) in a single day. He uses a helicopter to shuttle him between the climbs.

July 1985: Ken Evans and Matt Christensen climb Rainier from Paradise to summit in 3:44. They use running shoes and ski poles the entire way up the glacier route. They do the round trip in 5:09.

1986: Erhard Loretan and Jean Troillet simul-solo the North Face Direct on Everest in less than two days basecamp-to-basecamp. They pioneer a bold style of "night naked-ness" by climbing without bivouac gear, ropes, harness, protection, etc. They climb mostly at night to stay warm and rest during daylight hours. They glissade the entire face from summit to base in a mere five hours.

June 1986: John Bachar and Peter Croft climb the Nose (10:05) and the Regular Northwest Face of Half Dome (4:05) in a single 18-hour day. This is the first link-up of two grade VI walls in a day.

1988: Marc Batard is the first to climb Everest in a single day (less than 24 hours from base camp to summit). The route was previously prepared and it was not a complete solo ascent.

Summer 1988: Steve Schneider and Romain Vogler climb the Nose and the West Face in 23 hours. This is the first time El Cap is climbed twice in one day.

May 1989: Steve Schneider becomes the first person to solo the Nose in a day. He completes the route in 21:22.

Summer 1990: Alain Ghersen enchains the American Direct Route on the Dru with Walker Spur on the Grandes Jorasses and the Great Peuterey Ridge in a single 66-hour marathon.

Summer 1990: Catherine Destivelle solos the Bonatti Pillar on the Dru in five hours.

June 1990: Peter Croft and Dave Schultz climb the Nose and the Salathé in 18 hours. This is the first and still only time two grade VI El Cap routes have been climbed in a day.

July 1990: Derek Hersey free solos three routes (Yellow Wall with the Forest Finish 5.11, Casual Route 5.10, and Pervertical Sanctuary 5.10+), about 25 pitches of climbing, on the Diamond of Longs Peak before 11 A.M.

October 2, 1990: Wojciech Kurtyka, Jean Troillet, and Erhard Loretan climb a new route on South Face of Shishapangma in one day. They cut weight even further by carrying no bivouac gear and climbing at night—resting and brewing only during the warmer daylight hours.

October 1990: Steve Gerberding, Scott Stowe, and Rick Lovelace climb the North American Wall in 24:05. While missing the one-day ascent, they prove that hard aid routes can be done in a single push. They also establish the concept of a **push ascent** in contrast to a **one-day ascent.**

Spring 1991: Derek Hersey free solos three routes (Scenic Cruise, 5.10+; Journey Home 5.10+; and the Leisure Climb, 5.9) in a day.

Summer 1991: Derek Hersey solos up Scenic Cruise (5.10+), down Leisure Climb (5.9), and then up Journey Home (5.10+), all in the Black Canyon of the Gunnison in Colorado. These three routes total 30+ pitches of climbing. Hersey's route takes six hours car-to-car.

Summer 1991: Alex Lowe completes the Grand Traverse in 8:15.

Fall 1991: Charlie Fowler solos the 1800-meter Harlin Direct on the North Face of the Eiger in 14 hours roundtrip.

June 1992: Peter Croft and Hans Florine climb the Nose of El Capitan in 4:22. In the process they take simul-climbing to a new level when one of their "pitches" is 1,000-feet long!

July 1992: Peter Croft and Dave Schultz climb the Rostrum via Excellent Adventure (5.13b, 1:30), the Crucifix (5.12a, 3:30), West Face of El Cap (2:20), and the first three pitches of Astroman (through the first 5.11c pitch) in a day. This is the first time three grade V routes were linked in a day, free.

June 1993: On his first ever attempt at soloing, Hans Florine climbs the Nose in 14:10, cutting the solo speed record on the Nose by a third.

Summer 1994: Rolando Garibotti sets the speed records on Lurking Fear (with Jon Rosmengy) and the Shield (with Adam Wainright). This is the first prevalent use of **short-fixing technique** to Yosemite speed climbing.

October 1994: Steve Schneider and Hans Florine climb the Nose, Lurking Fear, and the West Face in 23:01. It is the first and only time three El Cap routes have been done in a day.

Fall 1995: Steve Gerberding, Scott Stowe, and Dave Bengston climb the sustained and difficult Pacific Ocean Wall in 36:24. This route was originally rated A5 and becomes the most difficult route ever climbed in a single push.

Summer 1998: Dean Potter becomes the center of the speed climbing world with an almost ropeless ascent of the Regular Northwest Face of Half Dome in 4:17. While not pioneering the technique of **ropeless climbing as a means to speed,** Potter takes it into the 5.11 range with big exposure on Half Dome and the Nose.

Summer 1998: Dean Potter sets a host of records with Jose Pereyra including the Salathé Wall (7:33), Lurking Fear (7:15). They pioneer the **use of a Ropeman (microascender) to protect the leader from a second falling off while simul-climbing**, though it still hasn't been that widely used.

Summer 1998: Dean Potter climbs Royal Arches (15 pitches, 5.7 A0) in 57 minutes car-to-car and Snake Dike in three hours car-to-car. This starts an interest in **fast roundtrip ascents of moderate routes**, which involve running on the approach and the descent.

August 1998: Mike Pennings and Topher Donahue climb Pervertical Sanctuary (5.10+) on the Diamond, solo the North Ridge (5.6) on Spearhead, climb the South Face (5.8) of the Petit Grepon, do the first post-massive-rockfall ascent of the Northcutt-Carter route (5.10) on Hallet Peak's north face, and then climb the Spiral Route (5.4) on Notchtop by headlamp. They start at 3 A.M. from the Longs Peak parking lot and finish at the Bear Lake parking lot at 1:30 A.M. the next day.

April 1999: Mike Pennings and Jeff Hollenbaugh link the Touchstone Wall, Space Shot, Monkeyfinger Wall, and Moonlight Buttress in Zion National Park in 18 hours.

Summer 1999: Dean Potter solos the Casual Route on Longs Peak in a car-to-car time of four hours. This involves a 3,500-vertical-foot approach and then 1,500 feet of up to 5.10 climbing at an elevation of 14,000 feet.

July 26–28, 1999: Dean Potter becomes the first to solo the Nose (in a record time of just under 13 hours) and the Regular Northwest

Face of Half Dome in a day. Potter makes heavy use of "leaver-biners" to protect himself while roped climbing, but eliminates the need to descend and clean the gear. With Potter's feat unbeknownst to him, Hans Florine links the same two routes, in reverse order, in 21:40 (setting the solo record of 3:57 on Half Dome in the process).

October 1999: Hans Florine and Jim Herson simul-climb the Regular Northwest Face of Half Dome in 1:53. Herson leads the entire 22-pitch route without ever getting within 100 feet of Florine and they re-gear only once (by hauling it up on the rope).

May 21, 2000: Babu Chiri Sherpa climbs Everest from Nepal base camp to summit in record time of 16:56.

Summer 2000: Hans Florine solos Lurking Fear and the West Face in a day. It is the first time two El Cap routes have been soloed in a day.

August 26, 2000: Rolando Garibotti solos the Grand Traverse in the Tetons in 6:40, breaking Alex Lowe's mythical time.

September 2000: Teddy Keizer (aka Cavedog) climbs all 54 Colorado 14ers in 10 days, 20 hours, and 26 minutes, breaking the one-year-old previous record by nearly two days!

November 2000: Steve Edwards ascends 400 boulder problems in a day in the Santa Barbara area as part of his 40 days of birthday challenges leading up to his 40th.

June 2001: Steve House and Rolando Garibotti climbed Alaska's Infinite Spur, a 9,000-foot sweep of granite and ice, in a blistering fast 25 hours. The fastest previous climb was seven days.

APPENDIX 1
SPEED BETA FOR SPECIFIC ROUTES

Obsessed with the Nose
by Hans Florine

The lifetime goal of many climbers is to simply climb El Capitan in Yosemite Valley. El Cap is probably the most highly sought after and widely climbed big wall in the world. The reasons are obvious: great weather, no approach, relatively easy descent, perfect rock, variety of lines, etc. Bill and I have a total of 39 ascents on the Nose between us.

For aspiring speed climbers the lifetime goal is not just to climb El Cap, but to climb it in a day. While the East Buttress (5.10b, 12 pitches) is clearly on El Cap, it doesn't seem to receive the same distinction as the other routes because it is easy going and short. Although other routes like Mr. Midwest (near the West Face) and the Shortest Straw (near the East Buttress) are just as short, they have a level of difficulty that puts them into the "real El Cap route" category.

One of the easiest "real El Cap routes" on the main monolith is also the most famous. It is in the center, it takes the longest straight line, and it is the line of the first ascent—the Nose. "Nose in a day" (NIAD) is practically a trademarked phrase for speed climbing. It is the feather in every true speed climber's cap. It is the rite of passage, the coup de grâce, the ante-up, and the badge of honor. The Nose follows beautiful cracks, towers, flakes, and corners. It is considered by many to be the greatest pure rock climb in the world. The Nose is relatively free of the scary and physically demanding wide cracks that populate the Salathé, yet has hundreds of feet of fun 5.7 to 5.10 cracks. Heck, the route even goes free at 5.13c/d.

A brief history of fast ascents on the Nose. The first ascent in 1958 took 12 days, and the final push was made by Wayne Mary, James Whitmore, and Warren Harding. In 1960 the first "single push ascent" took six days and was accomplished by Joe Fitschen, Chuck Pratt, Tom

Frost, and Royal Robbins. In 1963 a team of three climbed the route in three and a half days. In 1975 the route received its first "one-day" ascent. By the late 1980s numerous teams had done the route in less than a half day, with an Austrian team having done it in nine hours and change. In 1989 Steve Schneider climbed the Nose in under 24 hours solo!

Things got heated in the early 1990s. Steve Schneider and I (H.F.) set the record at 8:05 in 1990. The following week Peter Croft and Dave Shultz did a staggering job of dropping the time to 6:40! In the spring of 1991, Andres Puhvel and I lowered the time to 6:03. The following week Peter and Dave blew everyone's minds with a time of 4:48! In the spring of 1992, Peter Croft and I set the speed record on the Nose at 4:22, which was still standing as of September 2001. Interestingly, that same day in 1992, Nancy Feagin and Sue McDevit did the first one-day ascent of the Nose by an all female team. I set the solo record in 1993 at 14:11; and Dean Potter made it solo in under 13 hours in 1999, then he went over and climbed Half Dome the same day!

Beta for your NIAD trip. The tricks used to get a sub-six-hour time are extreme and not for most climbers. Not for most speed climbers, in fact. How about the "aspiring speed climber?" Can they also climb the Nose in a day? Yes! A solid 5.10 free climber can climb the Nose in a day. While I don't consider 5.10 crack climbing to be easy, the NIAD is within range of an average weekend warrior who puts in the training and the mileage.

First, do your homework. Work up to a route this big. The Nose is 31 pitches and just shy of 3,000 feet. (If you stretch a 60-meter rope each time, it's 21 pitches, zero simul-climbing.) Try to do a 1,000-foot wall in a day (West Face of Leaning Tower or South Face of Washington Column). Then do a 2,000-foot wall (Northwest Face of Half Dome). Get familiar with the "Big Stone." Do the East Buttress and learn the East Ledges Descent. Do the West Face in a day. Do the Nose in two or three days to learn the route. Climb it again to learn the variations.

Rest for a day or two before the attempt. Make the attempt in June when the days are long and the weather is predictable. You'll go faster with a little extra water weight in the daylight (hot summer days) than you would going lighter (with less water) and climbing in the dark in October. Get to bed early the night before and start climbing the next day at 4:30 A.M. Starting this early maximizes daylight and hopefully reduces night climbing at the end of the day.

The lead line. How long of a lead line? You can use a 50-, 60-, or 70-

meter rope. See the detailed topo and read over the information in Chapter 4 about rope selection. I recommend a 60-meter lead line, but there are uses for a 70-meter line if you can conserve gear and stretch it that far—and if you don't mind the extra 10 meters of rope weight.

The rack. The rack for the Nose is largely dependent on the skill and boldness of the leaders. Peter Croft is comfortable running it out 50 feet on 5.10 hand or fist jamming, but the average 5.10 climber will not do this. You might calculate leading with gear every 10 feet when the going is 5.10, every 15 feet at 5.9, and every 20 feet or more when the going is easier. Gear is necessary every 3 to 5 feet when aiding, but the leader can aggressively back clean. These calculations make for a large rack.

You can bring one set of RP's and one set of stoppers, although I've done the whole route placing only one nut. Bring two sets of cams up to 2.5 inches, triples of all could be useful. Selectively, triple up on the .5-, 1-, and 2-inch cams, and bring one each of 3-, 3.5-, and 4-inch. Consider two #3s and two #4s if you *really* suck at off-widths. The biggest pieces can ride in the pack most of the time. Bring 12 quick draws and four to six over-the-shoulder slings with two biners for each (I like to keep these triple looped so they look, ride, and act like quick draws). Bring two lightweight etriers/aiders and daisy chains (these too can ride in pack most of the way). The second will need ascenders and JJs, foot loops, or etriers.

Passing other parties. Undoubtedly, you'll have to pass other parties. This route is extremely popular and I've seen up to nine parties climbing the route at the same time. If the route is overly crowded, you might opt to try another day. Passing is practically mandatory so be prepared for that. See Chapter 6 for passing strategies.

Leading in blocks. The route should be led in blocks. Each climber should clip into the lead line with two locking biners. Not tying directly to the rope allows for quick switching of rope ends. It is best to switch leaders at a good ledge to make the logistics of the changeover easier. Some natural places to switch leaders include Sickle Ledge, Dolt Tower, El Cap Tower, Texas Flake, Boot Flake, Camp IV, Camp V, and Camp VI. Keeping the same leader the whole way is the fastest method.

Pitch by pitch. Approach the 1st pitch via the 5.7 route "Pine Line" to the left or up the 5th class scramble on the right. Pine Line is more direct and easier for hauling (not that you are hauling, are you?) but more technically difficult. Start your watch when you take off from the ledge at the base of the 1st pitch! (All pitches referred to from here on are as per the topo on pages 112–113.)

You should be able to complete the route in 19 to 32 pitches. If it takes you 24 pitches, you need to average 60 minutes a pitch to do the NIAD. Best of luck!

Pitch 1: This pitch is demanding of your free climbing skills. It is one of the few places on the route where you can't easily aid past free moves. Keep an eye out to the right for footholds that help upward progress. All size cams work on this pitch.

Pitch 2: This pitch keeps the heat on. You need to pull off a couple free moves with flaring pro placements just prior to grabbing the pendulum point and swinging right to the next crack. Save your 1- to 2-inch cams to leapfrog in the flaring pin scars after the pendulum.

Advanced Tips (AT): You'll need a 70-meter rope to combine the 1st and 2nd pitch. If you simul-climb either one, remember to have the first "pull" the second up in a counterweight fashion when he lowers for the pendulum.

Pitch 3: This pitch contains more flaring cracks, but bomber placements abound after running it 30 feet off the belay. A 2-bolt, bolt ladder takes you to fixed gear and another bolt, then French freeing this last bolt gets you to 15 feet of 5.9+ climbing and the belay.

AT: You'll need 60.5 meters to combine the 2nd and 3rd pitch.

Pitch 4: This pitch takes you to Sickle Ledge. Climb 15 feet of 5.5–5.6 to a smooth corner; then a single hook move or a 5.10+ stem gains a 1-inch cam placement in a flaring pin scar. After one more flared cam placement, you'll gain fixed gear and bolts, which leads to the first pendulum point. Clip in high to this pendulum piece and lower out slowly to tension traverse over to the 2-inch, right-facing corner. Pull against this until you can reach up to the fixed swing point here; clip it and swing right for the big ledge that is on the left side of Sickle Ledge. Tall people can stem from the 2-inch, right-facing corner to the huge flake that marks the left side of Sickle. If you are trailing a rope, watch out for the rope-eating flake on the far left side of Sickle, down about 50 feet.

Sickle Ledge is considered to be one-tenth of the way up the route. Fractional marks will be given so you can check your time and see how you're doing. These fractions are *not* length in distance climbed but the time consumed at that point for a day ascent. For example, if it takes you and your partner three hours to get to Sickle, your team will likely take 30 hours to complete the route. If you only have supplies for a 14-hour ascent, you should consider backing off.

Pitch 5: Scramble up 4th class and 5.4 over to the upper right side of Sickle Ledge.

Pitch 6: This pitch is 5.5 leading up to a short steep 5.9+ crack that takes you out around the corner onto the face where a bolted belay awaits you.

AT: From the big chain anchors on Sickle, it is 62 meters to the end of the 6th pitch, just out of the top of Sickle. With a tiny bit of simul-climbing, you can combine the 5th pitch (4th class) with the 6th pitch (5.9). The second is on easy 4th class terrain, while the leader is going up the 5.6 and 5.9.

Pitch 7: Lower off the anchor about 40 or more feet and swing over to the left-facing corner that leads up to Dolt Hole. Climb as high as you feel comfortable before placing gear to make it easier on the follower when they lower over. Put in the belay about 20 feet down from Dolt Hole.

(Note: Get out the big gear for pitch 8–14.)

Pitch 8 (B variation per topo): Lower down to tension traverse right along the bolted 5.10d variation. You are now in the Stovelegs. Do *not* go one more crack to the right! Again, climb as high as you feel comfortable before putting in protection. This .75- to 1.5-inch lieback crack leads into the most beautiful 2-inch hand jamming section of the route. After 80 feet of 5.8 hand jamming, you'll reach a 3-inch crack and then a fixed bong and a new ⅜-inch bolt for a belay. These are at a turn in the crack and before the crack gets small again.

AT (pitch 5–8): Simul-climb pitch 5 and 6 as suggested earlier. When the leader lowers off the 6th anchor to do the tension traverse, have him "pull" the second up in a counterweight fashion. Keep simul-climbing while the leader is going up the dihedral to Dolt Hole. If the second needs a belay for the final 15 feet to the 6th belay, then the leader can slam in a couple of pieces and belay the second on that section before continuing.

About 20 feet below Dolt Hole, you'll find a ¼-inch bolt, often with tat on it, on the face 5 feet right of the crack. Clip this bolt and do

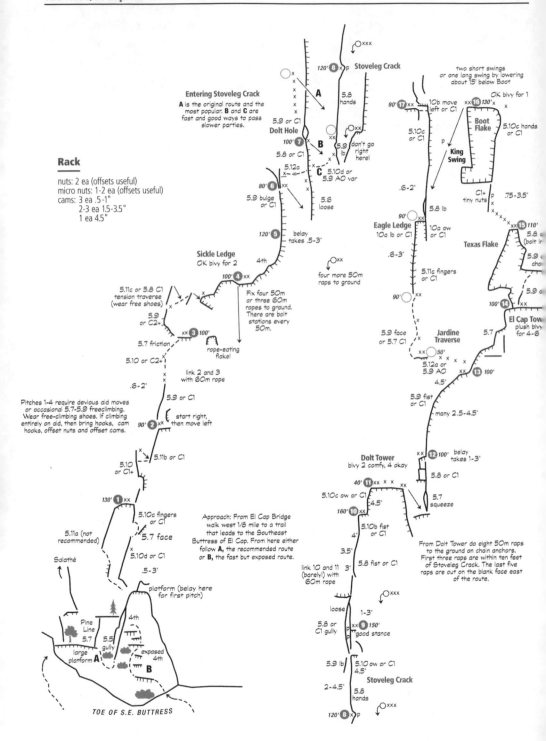

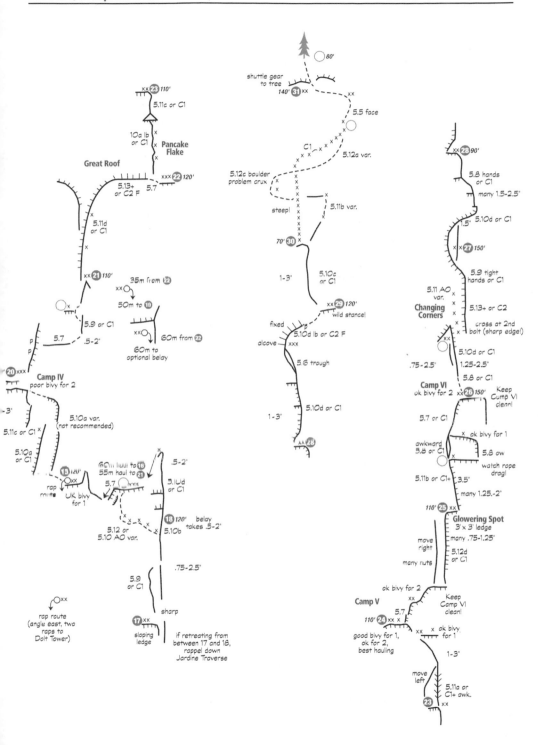

xx **23** 110'

5.11c or C1

10a lb
or C1

**Pancake
Flake**

Great Roof

5.13+   5.7
or C2 F

xxx **22** 120'

5.11d
or C1

xx **21** 110'

35m from **22**

xx

50m to **19**

5.9 or C1

5.7   .5-2"

xx

60m from **22**

60m to
optional belay

20 xxx

Camp IV
poor bivy for 2

-3"

5.10a var.
(not recommended)

5.11c or C1

5.10a
or C1

19 120'

xx

60m haul to **18**
55m haul to **21**

.5-2"

rap
route

UK bivy
for 1

5.7

5.10d
or C1

18 120'   belay
takes .5-2"

5.12 or
5.10 AO var.

5.10b

.75-2.5"

5.9
or C1

xx

rap route
(angle east, two
raps to
Dolt Tower)

sharp

17 xx

sloping
ledge

if retreating from
between 17 and 18,
rappel down
Jardine Traverse

80'

shuttle gear
to tree

140' **31** xx

xx

5.5 face

C1

5.12a var.

5.12c boulder
problem crux

5.11b var.

steep!

70' **30**

1-3"

5.10c
or C1

xx **29** 120'
wild stance!

fixed

alcove

5.10d lb or C2 F

xxx

5.6 trough

1-3"

5.10d or C1

28

5.5 face

xx **28** 90'

5.8 hands
or C1

many 1.5-2.5"

5.10d or C1

x **27** 150'

5.9 tight
hands or C1

5.11 AO
var.

**Changing
Corners**

5.13+ or C2

cross at 2nd
bolt (sharp edge!)

xx

5.10d or C1

.75-2.5"   1.25-2.5"

5.8 or C1

Camp VI
ok bivy for 2 xx **26** 150'   Keep
Camp VI
clean!

5.7 or C1

x ok bivy for 1

awkward
5.8 or C1

5.8 ow

watch rope
drag!

5.11b or C1+   3.5"

many 1.25-2"

110' **25** xx

Glowering Spot
3' x 3' ledge

many .75-1.25"

move
right

5.12d
or C1

many nuts

ok bivy for 2

Camp V

xx   5.7

110' **24** xx x

good bivy for 1,
ok for 2,
best hauling

xx x ok bivy
for 1

1-3"

move
left

5.11a or
C1+ awk.

23 xx

Keep
Camp VI
clean!

another tension traverse over to the very bottom of the Stovelegs. Continue up the Stoveleg crack until you run out of rope. With a 60-meter rope, you'll be able to reach the 8th belay while the second is still at the 6th anchor. Remember, after each pendulum try to wait as long as possible to put in your first piece or the rope drag will kill you and the follower will have a harder time lowering out. With this method the rope is stretched tight; the second will need a lower out line. Either bring a 110-foot length of 7/8-millimeter rope or a full 60-meter length to use in case retreat is needed.

You can combine pitch 7 and 8 without simul-climbing. However, it's possible to lower off the 6th anchor while belaying the climber in the Stovelegs and continue simuli-climbing until the leader runs out of gear. Peter and I simul-climbed all the way to the top of pitch 16 from the top of pitch 4!

(Note: This is a good area to pass another party. Because there are three ways to move from the Dolt Hole crack system to the Stovelegs, it is possible to go around a slower party here without impeding their climbing.)

Pitch 9–11: These three pitches up to Dolt Tower can be combined into two pitches with a 60-meter rope. Just run out the rope and construct a belay from gear or fixed pieces wherever you end up. The last 130 feet to the top of Dolt Tower is a great place to leapfrog a #3 and #4 cam. You've got to keep them with you until the end unless you bring two of each. On top of Dolt Tower, you are one-quarter of the way up the route. If you planned on a 14-hour ascent and it took you eight hours to get here, you better consider backing off. (Convenient 50-meter rap stations lead to the ground from here.)

Pitch 12: The leader lowers off the right side of Dolt Tower and then goes up the 5.9 crack. After wrestling in a wide flaring chimney crack, you'll reach great bear hugging cracks that are side by side. Transfer to the right one as you near the anchor, which is a fixed pin and two nice ⅜-inch bolts. The leader should back clean low on this pitch to make the swing or lower out easier for the follower. This creates for less rope drag and makes it easier to combine the next pitch. The second either lowers out on the fixed line (that is usually there) or the lower-out line, or easily downclimbs and crosses to the crack.

Pitch 13: This is a well-protected crack to a 3- to 4-inch corner crack up to a large ledge. The pitch ends with a bolted belay at the base of the Jardine traverse.

AT: You'll need 56 meters to combine pitch 12 and 13. Once at the top of the 13th pitch, you can put away the big gear until pitch 26, but keep out one 3.5-inch cam.

(Note: Most parties take a long time to deal with pitches 14–19. Consider taking the Jardine variation to the left at the top of pitch 13. It is faster than going on the original route.)

Pitch 14: Combine the 14th pitch up to El Cap Tower with the Texas Flake pitch with easy simul-climbing or just go to El Cap Tower. Belay from El Cap Tower or from the front of Texas Flake.

Pitch 15: Climb the Texas Flake by facing out and on the west side of the flake (west side of the route). You can reach around and grab the front of the flake once you get up high enough. The Texas Flake pitch now has a bolt that protects the chimney somewhat, but unfortunately the bolt is on the east side. It's best not to clip the bolt so you can then flip the rope to the outside of the flake allowing the follower the luxury of not having to jug inside the flake. The top of this flake is one-third of the way up the route.

Pitch 16: This is the Boot Flake, an easy bolt ladder to a thin and slowly widening crack—easy to French free.

AT: You can combine pitch 16 with the Texas Flake pitch. It is less than 60 meters from the base of the Texas to the top of the Boot. Or, do it with some simul-climbing, which isn't as radical as it seems. The Texas Flake pitch requires (or even allows for) little gear. This leaves you plenty for the next pitch, which is half bolt ladder and half thin hand crack. While the leader is climbing the 5.10c hands or the bolt ladder, the second is climbing the relatively easy ground up to the Texas Flake and doing the chimney behind.

Pitch 17: Do the King Swing by lowering down until you're 15 feet below the bottom of Boot Flake. Run to the right first and take one long swing into the corner and crack, which leads into the gray bands. The leader must now back clean all the gear while leading up to the 17th belay anchor and beyond. The safest way to do this is for the leader to lead as high as comfortable without gear, place gear normally until the rope drag gets bad, and then place a couple of bomber pieces and lower down to clean the bottom pieces. Lather, rinse, and repeat. The leader continues this strategy up to the 17th belay anchor.

Pitch 18: Lead up to the right side of the ledge that the 19th belay anchor is on.

AT: You can keep stretching the lead after the King Swing to the top of the 19th pitch or to the right side of the ledge that the 19th belay anchor is on. The second follows this pitch by lowering out on a lower line or with the remaining rope end. The leader must stop at (or between) the belay for pitch 17 and 18 if you have no lower out line because the follower will need all the extra rope for the lower out. After the King Swing I try to wait until above the 17th belay to leave my first piece of protection. This makes the lower out a ton easier for the follower.

AT (pitch 15–17): Here's beta for the "super advanced." Have the leader back clean or solo leaving *no gear* from the heel to the top of the Boot. When the follower arrives at the heel of the Boot, she clips in and switches from jugging to being on the end of the rope. She also sends the jugs up to the previous leader on top of the Boot, and the leader sends down the rest of the rack if it wasn't left at the heel already. The leader puts the follower on belay and the follower does the King Swing. *Bam!* You've eliminated the follower going to the top of the boot, you've eliminated having to lower someone back down 70 feet, and you've switched leaders.

Pitch 19: For this pitch get up to the ledge via the bolted face climbing or go up cracks and lower down onto the ledge, then traverse left on 4th class, execute one 5.7 downclimb move, and scamper over to a bolted belay.

Pitch 20-21: Climb up 5.11c or A0 to Camp IV, then continue on 100 feet of 5.9 up and over to the base of the Great Roof pitch. These two pitches can be combined into one. It is less than 60 meters from the 19th belay anchor to the 21st. When the follower goes past Camp IV, you're at the halfway point. You want to be here in well under 12 hours for the NIAD.

AT: Have the second cruise across the ledge that anchor 19 is on while the leader is going up pitch 20. Consider short-fixing to Camp IV and self-belay leading up pitch 21 while the follower is jugging.

Pitch 22: Although pitch 22 is only 110 feet, it takes a bunch of gear and time. Leapfrog ⅜-, ½-, and ¾-inch cams, and clip the fixed pins and nuts.

Pitch 23: This pitch is spectacular and has possibly the best lieback crack in the world. It would be a shame not to free this 70 feet of glory. A few 1-inch cam placements and clipping fixed pieces gets you through it to a nice triangle ledge. Here, a very thin section leads up; use the smallest cams you have and small nuts until the crack widens to ¾- and 1-inch. About 20 feet of 5.7 ledge-mantling leads to the bolted anchors.

AT: Upon reaching the 22nd belay anchor, pull up all the slack, fix the rope, and self-belay lead the Pancake Flake while the follower is jugging/cleaning the 22nd pitch. From the triangle ledge at the top of the Pancake Flake, you can reach Camp V in one rope length.

Pitch 24: On this pitch keep an eye out for a place where you can get out of the flaring corner and reach into the nice 1-inch crack on the left. Things move faster out of the flare. End pitch 24 on any of the Camp V ledges because pitch 25 is pretty short.

Pitch 25: This is a tough aid or free lead (thin nut placements). Keep an eye out for a place where you can get into the crack on your right in the corner. Leapfrogging cams in this crack goes faster than tinkering in the seam.

Pitch 26: On this pitch be ready to leapfrog your 1-inch, then 2-inch, and finally 3- and 4-inch cams. If you're up for it, this pitch is a wonderful, albeit hard, 5.10+ hand crack to free climb. Stay on the left side of all the blocky ledges up to Camp VI.

AT: Haul up some line when you reach the Glowering Spot and fix the rope. Lead on self-belay up pitch 26 while the follower is cleaning pitch 25.

Pitch 27: Eighty feet off Camp VI you can go into the dihedral on the right down low or higher after going up the 5.11 sport bolts on the left. If you're six feet or taller, the sport bolts can be French freed at 5.11a. It's much faster than aiding the dihedral.

AT: If you led to the very end of a 60-meter rope every time from Camp VI up (regardless of where you belayed), you'd be off in 3 pitches.

Pitch 28: This is an easy hand crack. Leapfrog with 1- and 2-inch pieces if not freeing the pitch.

Pitch 29: This pitch eats up pieces from .75 to 1.5 inches.

Pitch 30: A tricky face move gets you into the crack, this pitch is fun 5.10 liebacking and very short.

Pitch 31: This pitch takes a bunch of draws, definitely back clean every other one. If you skip more than that, you risk making it hard for the second to clean. The easy hauling anchor is a nice airy spot—definitely worth a pause to gape down the route.

AT: Pitch 30 and 31 are short enough to combine; however, rope drag can easily foil that plan. Consider short-fixing the lead rope 25 feet above where it turns the lip and self-belay from there to the top while your partner is jugging the steep bolted section. From the bolts at the 31st belay, you can walk up slabs to a tree and celebrate in the shade. (Unless you topped out in the dark!) These bolts are where a NIAD time is considered stopped (as per every reported ascent I know of).

Beta on the Yellow Spur
by Bill Wright

The Yellow Spur was first ascended by Colorado icon Layton Kor and Dave Dornan in 1959. With seven pitches, it is one of the longer routes in Eldorado; and local guidebook author, Richard Rossiter, lists it as one of his top ten routes on the Redgarden Wall. The Yellow Spur, rated 5.9, but with 5.10b/c variations, is an extremely popular route. A speed ascent of this route can take three approaches: swinging leads (because it is a free climb), simul-climbing (if the climbers are comfortable at this level), or free soloing.

Swinging leads on the Yellow Spur. The 1st pitch of the Yellow Spur passes a large roof. The traditional 5.9 start begins in a right-facing dihedral, then the route climbs up to the roof where it traverses directly left before turning the lip. Once above the lip the route goes directly back to the right. Rope drag is an issue and long slings are recommended. This pitch, because of the twists and turns and the difficult crux, is rarely combined with the next pitch. The belay is at a tree with slings. A direct 5.10b/c start avoids the first traverse to the left and goes directly over the roof. This is shorter and a bit faster, but the climbing is tricky and the gear is strenuous to place.

You can combine the 2nd (5.8) and 3rd (5.7) pitch easily with a 50-

Yellow Spur

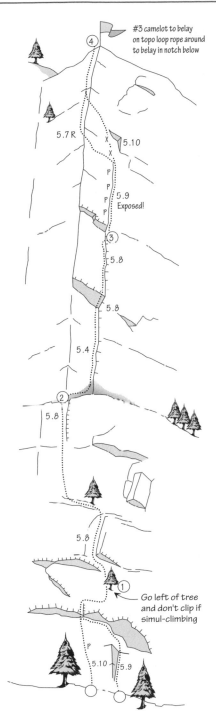

#3 camelot to belay
on topo loop rope around
to belay in notch below

④

5.7 R

X
X
5.10

P
P
P
P

5.9
Exposed!

③

5.8

5.8

5.4

②

5.8

5.8

①

Go left of tree
and don't clip if
simul-climbing

P

5.10   5.9

Credit: Greg Opland

meter rope. The belay at the top of the 3rd pitch is a 3-foot ledge. This is a good place to stop because the next pitch traverses. The 4th pitch is easy (5.4) and traverses directly right on this ledge, then goes up a corner system to a ledge. Don't stop here, continue by the 5.8 roof above. Make a tricky move protected with small gear and head out to a stance on the arête to belay.

The best pitch of the route looms above and provides stellar, balance intensive 5.9 climbing protected by a slew of fixed pitons. Once up this section the leader can either head out left on exciting, unprotected ground (5.8) or forge straight up past a couple of bolts (5.10b). Both lines are recommended, so come back and do the route a second time. After this section, no matter which variation you follow, head up the exposed, unprotected 5.6 arête to the summit. You've just done a speed ascent of Yellow Spur!

Simul-climbing the Yellow Spur. Simul-climbing can be such a joyous pursuit with the right partner. It is like climbing with a super long rope. No need to stop climbing after only 50 meters, just keep going until you are out of gear. The latter is certainly a concern. Frequently when simul-climbing you'll need a bigger than average rack. It all depends on the boldness of the climbers and on how long you want to go before regrouping.

To do the Yellow Spur as one pitch, you'll need about twice the normal rack. The key to simul-climbing the Yellow Spur is to minimize rope drag and protect the team from the tricky sections. To this end, once the leader clears the roof on the 1st pitch, he should place a micro-ascender to ensure that if his second falls on this crux section, it won't pull him off.

After traversing over to the belay tree, make sure to pass the tree on the left side and don't clip this belay. Then climb up and left over relatively easy ground to the base of the 2nd pitch dihedral. Place gear here. Be careful because a fall from this point will probably land you on the ground. Whenever I run out a long section, I like to place two pieces before moving on.

Try not to place gear too close to the top of the 3rd pitch so that the rope runs smoother over to the 4th pitch dihedral. At the roof on the 5th pitch, if you place gear at the start of this roof, consider putting two slings on it. Finally, at the top of the crux section on the 6th pitch, place a second micro-ascender. Using the micro-ascenders in this manner frees the leader from the danger of the second falling on 5.9 or 5.10 terrain. Of course, falling at any time while simul-climbing is extremely serious; and if either team member is not solid at this level, regular belayed climbing should be used.

For an all out speed ascent, I'd recommend both the direct start and the direct finish. You might find it strange that I'd recommend the harder variations when trying to go fast. I recommend these variations for speed if free climbing is not a concern. By liberally grabbing and pulling on gear, French freeing, you can move through these sections fast. In particular, the delicate 5.9 climbing on the 6th pitch can go extremely fast. It all depends on what type of experience you're after.

Rack for swinging leads. Single camming units from blue Alien size through #2 Camalot; a set of stoppers (no RP's are required for this route—an Eldorado rarity); six quick draws; and six shoulder-length slings. Take a #3 Camalot to use for the belay on the summit.

Rack for simul-climbing. If you simul-climb right past the summit and down into the notch, the #3 Camalot used for the belay on top is not necessary because you can loop the rope around the summit spire—it works perfectly as a top piece. Because you're doing the route as one pitch, you need more gear. Thankfully, the route has a number of fixed pieces, and the only crucial aspect is lots of quick draws and slings. I recommend 20 draws/slings to do this route as one simul-climbed pitch, and even then you'll have to run it out in places. I'd double up on all the camming units. Also, two micro-ascenders will add to the security.

Pitch 1: Clip 3–4 quick draws to fixed gear to turn the roof, then place a piece (red Alien) above the roof with a micro-ascender on it; clip slings at 1st belay.

Pitch 2: Place 3–4 pieces.

Pitch 3: Place 3–4 pieces; don't place anything near the top in order to reduce the rope drag in the traverse.

Pitch 4: Clip fixed sling at bottom of dihedral.

Pitch 5: Place one piece at the start of roof, clip the pin at the lip, and place one piece (small camming unit) to protect the hard move above.

Pitch 6: Clip all the fixed gear and place another micro-ascender once past the crux.

Pitch 7: Place one piece halfway up the arête, then either loop rope around the top spire or place a #3 Camalot.

APPENDIX 2
SPEED RECORDS

It's a Record!

It seems that anywhere there is a landmark mountain, no matter the difficulty of the route, be it hiking terrain or technical rock climbing, there is a speed record for the ascent. The Canadians track perhaps the most hilarious speed record. The beautiful, multi-turreted Castle Mountain has a small alpine hut 1,500 feet below the summit on the airy plateau. It is 3,000 vertical feet above the trailhead. The reported round-trip record for descending from the hut, driving to the liquor store, and returning is around 2 hours and 40 minutes.

The Web site for Yosemite speed climbing records is www.speedclimb. com, links to other areas are on this site as well. Colorado speed records have not been as meticulously recorded or as avidly pursued as Yosemite big wall records. Nevertheless, some times have been recorded through guidebooks and through word of mouth. The site www.wwwright.com/Climbing/ColoradoSpeed.html is an attempt to keep a more formal record of local speed climbs. E-mail in your ascents!

Speed Records

El Capitan

Mr. Midwest:

7:40 Jacqueline Florine, Steve Schneider, and Hans Florine; August 2001.

Mirage:

20:02 Steve Gerberding, Dave Bengston, and Al Swanson; 1995

West Face:

1:56:16 Timmy O'Neill and Hans Florine; November 1999.

5:56 Lisa Coleman-Puhvel and Hans Florine; October 1998 (fastest female/male ascent).

8:16 Hans Florine—solo; June 2000 (soloed two El Cap routes in a day).

Realm of the Flying Monkeys:

9:59 Peter Coward and Hans Florine; July 1999.

Lurking Fear:

4:27 Jason Singer and Cedar Wright; June 2001.

9:20 Hans Florine—solo; June 2000 (soloed two El Cap routes in a day).

West Buttress:

13:42 Chandlee Harrel and Hans Florine; July 2000.

20:08 Kevin Thaw—solo; September 1996.

For Your Eyes Only (aka Octopussy):

27:00 Steve Gerberding, John Harpole, and Dave Bengston; early 1990s.

Aquarian Wall:

23:20 Greg Murphy, Peter Coward, and Steve Schneider; mid 1990s.

Horse Chute:

27:07 Mark Deger, Kevin Thaw, and Steve Schneider; 1996.

Dihedral Wall:

22:04 Mike Ousley and Chris McNamara; July 1999.

The Salathé:

6:32 Jim Herson and Chandlee Harrell; July 1999 (free variation on pitch 24 and 32).

7:33 Dean Potter and Jose Pereyra; September 1998.

27:20 Sue McDevitt and Nancy Feagin (all female); June 1998.

23:20 Steve Schneider—solo; June 1992.

12:30 Nancy Feagin and Hans Florine; June 1992 (fastest female/male ascent).

35:00 Yuji Hirayama; September 1997 (fastest free ascent, onsight).

Son of Heart:

29:24 Peter Coward, Steve Schneider, and Hans Florine; September 1993.

Sunkist:

19:24 Mark Melvin, Steve Schneider, and Hans Florine; July 1999.

Flight of the Albatross:

14:50 Brad McCray, Hans Florine, and Kelly Simard; July 2001.

The Shield:

10:58 Cedar Wright and Chris McNamara; August 1999.

Muir:

19:57 Niles and Brian McCray; June 2001.

Triple Direct:

8:20 Adam Wainwright and Rolo Garibotti; mid 90s.

Grape Race:

13:25 Chris McNamara and Jose Pereyra; June 1999.

The Nose:

4:22 Peter Croft and Hans Florine; June 1992.

16:30 Abby Watkins and Vera Wong (all female ascent); 1996.

12:59 Dean Potter—solo; July 1999 (start of El Cap and Half Dome in a day).

23:46 Lynn Hill; 1994 (fastest free ascent).

8:40 Lynn Hill and Hans Florine; July 1992 (fastest female/male ascent).

Tribal Rite:

23:33 Steve Gerberding, Scott Stowe, and Dave Bengston; early 1990s.

New Dawn:

23:50 Willy and Damien Benegas; mid 1990s.

Wall of Early Morning Light:

25:05 Steve Gerberding, Dave Bengston, and Scott Stowe; mid 1990s.

Mescalito:

23:28 Dean Potter, Jose Pereyra, and Russ Mitrovich; October 1998.

Pacific Ocean Wall:

35:00 Steve Gerberding, Scott Stowe, and Dave Bengston;1995.

Wyoming Sheep Ranch:

29:31 Eric George, Russel Metrovich, and Sean "Stanley" Leary; October 1999.

North American Wall:

9:36 Tim O'Neill and Miles Smart; September 1999.

New Jersey Turn Pike:

16:09 Heather Bear, Steve Schneider, Hans Florine; August 2001.

Native Son:

25:06 Sean "Stanley" Leary, Russel Metrovich, and Eric George; October 1999.

Iron Hawk:

34:00 Dave Bengston, Scott Stowe, and Steve Gerberding; mid 1990s.

Aurora:

23:55 Miles Smart and Brian McCray; July 1998.

Tangerine Trip:

11:56 Miles Smart and Dean Potter; March 1999.

Lost in America:

21:31 Eric George, Russel Metrovich, and Leo Houlding; October 1999.

Kaos:

27:50 Jim Haden, Sean Leary, and Eric George; December 1999.

Zenyatta Mondatta:

26:25 Jose Peraya and Brian McCray; June 2001.

38:45 Willie Benegas—solo;1997.

Shortest Straw:

17:52 Russ Metrovich, Eric George, and Brett Dodds; September 1999.

Zodiac:

7:04 Chris McNamara and Miles Smart; March 1999.

12:00 Russ Metrovich—solo; August 1999.

Lunar Eclipse:

19:58 Ammon McNeely, Jose Pereyra, and Chongo; June 2001.

Bad Seed:

19:12 Wayne Wiloughby, Brian McCray, and Hans Florine; September 1998 (first one day ascent of El Cap by a handicapped person)!!

Eagles Way:

10:50 Cedar Wright, Tim O'Neill, and Miles Smart; August 1999 (rapped last pitch and cleaned pins after stopping clock).

19:05 Roxanne Brock and Brian McCray; August 1998 (fastest female/male ascent).

51:14 Ammon McNeely—solo; August 2000.

Water Fall Route:

18:28 Peter Coward, Steve Schneider, and Hans Florine; October 1997.

Chinese Water Torture:

17:15 Lance Allred, Steve Schneider, and Scott Stowe; early 1990s.

East Buttress:

00:43 Hans Florine—solo; July 2000 (2:09 car-to-car)!

2:20 Jason "Singer" Smith and Miles Smart; 1999 (car-to-car)!

1:30 Abby Watkins and Hans Florine; 1997 (3 hours even car-to-car)!

Half Dome Speed Ascents

Jet Stream:

18:50 Eric George, Russ Metrovich, and Jared Ogden; October 1999.

Tis-sa-ack:

12:00 Sean Kriletich and Jake Whitaker; 2000.

Direct Northwest Face:

8:20 Dean Potter and Jose Pereyra; 1998.

11:25 Miles Smart—solo; September 1999.

Regular North West Route:

1:53:25 Jim Herson and Hans Florine; October 1999.

9:45 Vera Wong and Abby Watkins; 1996.

5:40 Abby Watkins and Hans Florine; 1997 (fastest female/male ascent).

3:58 Hans Florine—solo; July 1999 (start of Half Dome and El Cap in a day).

Snake Dike:

3:00 Dean Potter; 1998 (car-to-car)!

Washington Column

Southern Man:

2:38 Cedar Wright and Jason Singer; June 2001.

South Face:

1:59 Cedar Wright and Dean Potter; March 2000.

Skull Queen:

2:59 Ammon McNeely and Cedar Wright; June 2000.

Astro Man:

1:30* Dean Potter or Peter Croft—solo; 2000 and 1988 respectively.
*Hans guessing at the time.

Reanimator:

11:56 Chris McNamara and Jacob Schmitz; June 1999.

The Prow:

3:01 Jason Singer and Cedar Wright; June 2001.

6:31 Willie Benegas—solo; October 1999.

Liberty Cap Regular Southwest Face:

9:31 Brian "Way" Knight and Rich Alburschkat; August 1993.

GLOSSARY

Many climbing terms are used in this book but are not included in this glossary. The terms that appear below are unique to, or prevalent in, efficient/speed climbing.

aiders: short for aid ladders; multi-step slings used for aid climbing; you clip an aider to a piece, then climb up the steps to place another piece. Often used interchangeably with etriers, yet not exactly the same thing.

batmanning: when a climber goes up the rope hand over hand like Batman and Robbin do on the side of a building.

bivy: short for the French word "bivouac," which means to sleep without shelter.

block: a collection of consecutive pitches on a long climb.

caterpillar technique: usually a method for a three-person team to climb a route. One person jugs a free line, one of the top two leads, and the third is cleaning the pitch below. This term gets confused with short-fixing by some (including Hans). See short fixing.

etrier: used instead of an aid ladder, the steps alternate on each side of a center piece of webbing.

flash: free climbing a route on your first attempt with the help of either some specific beta or watching someone else first.

follower: see second.

free solo: usually means an unroped free solo, but technically it could mean a roped (not aided) solo ascent.

Gri-Gri: a mechanical belay/rappel device that allows for hands-free belaying; manufacturer recommends that you keep a hand on the brake end of the rope.

in a day: doing an ascent "in a day" means that it took less than 24 hours, can be spread over two calendar days as Lynn Hill's "in a day" free ascent of the Nose.

leader: the first climber to ascend the pitch and place the protection.

leading in blocks: a way to climb that is frequently faster than swapping leads; the leader stays out in front for a set of pitches instead of switching every pitch.

leaver biner: a carabiner that is used and left behind; used while roped soloing so that the climber doesn't need to descend to retrieve them; also used for lowering out on a traverse.

NIAD: Nose In A Day.

nobivys: Hans' mantra and the essence of this book. Climbing without a bivouac.

onsight: climbing a route on your first attempt with no previous knowledge of the route, save the grade; more often applied to free climbing.

piece: any protection device such as nuts, camming units, pitons (aka pins), etc.

pinkpoint: free climbing a route with pre-placed gear and that you've attempted before; most sport climbers now call this a redpoint.

porta-ledge: portable cot-like structure that is hauled up a route, assembled, and attached to the rock in order to have a comfortable place to sleep.

push ascent: an ascent that is done without a bivy but takes longer than a normal climbing day, usually more than 24 hours.

redpoint: free climbing a route that you've attempted before; all gear must be placed on lead except for fixed gear such as bolts; climbers have equated this term to pinkpointing.

Reverso: a Petzl belay device used for belaying a leader or follower. Great for multi-tasking.

roped solo: soloing using a rope for protection.

second: also called follower; climber who follows the pitch and cleans the gear the leader has placed; the second and the leader frequently switch roles during a long climb.

short-fixing: a technique that allows the leader to get a jump on the next pitch by tying off the rope for the follower and continuing with a self-belay. See also caterpillar technique.

Silent Partner: a mechanical belay device used for roped solo climbing.

simul-climbing: roped climbing where both the leader and the other climber(s) on the rope are moving at the same time.

simul-seconding: a technique where the leader leads normally, sets up a belay, and belays two following climbers either on separate ropes or on the same rope; the followers are climbing at the same time.

simul-seconding on a single rope: same as simul-seconding except that both climbers are tied into the same rope; usually one climber is on the end of the rope and the other is tied in about 20 or 30 feet from the end.

simul-soloing: climbing unroped but with a partner; a technique frequently used in alpine climbing when ascending moderate couloirs or covering fourth class terrain; a common way to climb many of the classic Flatiron slab routes above Boulder, Colorado.

soloing: climbing alone, whether free or aid, roped or unroped; frequently used in place of the more descriptive "unroped free solo."

Soloist: a mechanical belay device used for roped solo climbing.

third classing: an unroped free solo; comes from the UIAA climbing classification that states a third class climb is a scramble that does not involve a rope; so when someone says he "third classed" a 5.10 route (which is class 5), it means that he climbed it as if it was third class (i.e., he didn't use a rope).

unroped solo: once meant unequivocally an unroped free solo, but with Russ Mitrovich's unroped aid solo of the Zodiac, it can only be taken to mean "climbing without a rope."

unroped free solo: climbing a route without a rope and freeing all the moves.

unroped French free solo: soloing without a rope and pulling on gear and/or aiding.

unroped aid solo: climbing a route using aid alone and without the use of a rope; *see* **unroped solo** and insane.

Wall Hauler: a combination pulley/camming device that makes hauling a bag much easier; indispensable when trying to haul the bag and belay the second at the same time; a Gri-Gri comes in handy as the belay device in this situation.

FURTHER READING
AND REFERENCES

Books

Anker, Daniel, ed. *Eiger: the Vertical Arena*. Seattle, Washington: The Mountaineers, 2000.

Arce, Gary. *Defying Gravity—High Adventure on Yosemite's Walls*. Berkeley, California: Wilderness Press, 1996.

Ardito, Stephano. *Mont Blanc*. Seattle, Washington: The Mountaineers, 1997.

Bridwell, Jim. *Climbing Adventures*. Merrillville, Indiana: ICS Books, 1992.

Brookfield, John. *Mastery of Hand Strength*. Ironmaid Enterprises, 1995.

Collister, Rob. *Lightweight Expeditions*. Ramsbury, Marlborough, England: The Crowood Press, 1989.

Duane, Dan. *El Capitan*. San Francisco, California: Chronicle Books, 2000.

Fanshawe, Andy, and Stephen Venables. *Himalaya Alpine-Style*. Seattle, Washington: The Mountaineers, 1995.

Frison-Roche, Roger, and Sylvain Jouty. *A History of Mountain Climbing*. New York, New York: Flammarion, 1996.

Godfrey, Robert, and Dudley Chelton. *Climb!* Boulder, Colorado: American Alpine Club, 1977.

Hepp, Tilmann, and Wolfgang Gullich. *A Life in the Vertical*. Stuttgart, Germany: Boulder Ed., 1994.

Jones, Chris. *Climbing in North America*. Berkeley, California: University of California Press, 1976.

Lee, Chip. *On Edge: The Life & Climbs of Henry Barber*. Boston, Massachusetts: Appalachian Mountain Club, 1982.

Long, John. *The High Lonesome*. Helena, Montana: Falcon Publishing, 1999.

_____. *Rock Jocks, Wall Rats and Hangdogs*. New York, New York: Fireside, 1994.

Long, John, and Craig Luebben. *Advanced Rock Climbing*. Conifer, CO: Chockstone Press, 1997.

Messner, Reinhold. *The Big Walls*. New York, New York: Oxford University Press, 1978.

Meyers, George. *Yosemite Climber*. Modesto, California: Diadem Books / Robbins Mountain Letters, 1979.

Meyers, George, and Don Reid. *Yosemite Climbs*. Denver, Colorado: Chockstone Press, 1987. (The history section of this edition of the Yosemite guidebook [by Meyers] is the best overall reference for free climbing history. Later editions by Reid [1995, 1999] do not include this section.)

Roper, Steve. *Camp 4*. Seattle, Washington: The Mountaineers, 1994.

_____. *Climber's Guide to Yosemite*. San Francisco, California: Sierra Club, 1971.

Roper, Steve, and Allen Steck. *Fifty Classic Climbs of North America*. San Francisco, California: Sierra Club, 1979.

Roth, Arthur. *Eiger: Wall of Death*. London, England: Victor Gollancz Ltd., 1982.

Rowell, Galen. *High and Wild*. San Francisco, California: Lexikos, 1983.

_____. *The Vertical World of Yosemite*. Berkeley, California: Wilderness Press, 1974.

Salkeld, Audrey. *World Mountaineering*. London, England: Octopus Publishing Group Ltd., 1998.

Scott, Chic. *Pushing the Limits*. Calgary, Alberta, Canada: Rocky Mountain Books, 2000.

Scott, Doug. *Big Wall Climbing*. London, England: Oxford University Press, 1974.

Twight, Mark F., and James Martin. *Extreme Alpinism*. Seattle, Washington: 1999.

Unsworth, Walt. *Savage Snows: The Story of Mont Blanc*. London, England: Hodder and Stoughton Limited, 1986.

Whymper, Edward. *Scrambles Amongst the Alps*. Berkeley, California: Ten Speed Press, 1981. (Originally published, 1871.)

Articles

Achey, Jeff. "Balancing Act." *Climbing* magazine 189 (1999): 74–81, 142–43.

Bridwell, Jim. "Brave New World." *Mountain* 31 (1973).

Duane, Dan. "Up on the Big Stone" *Outside Magazine* (October 2000): 80–88.

Gore, Peter. "The Unbeatable Body," *National Geographic* (September 2000): 32.

O'Neill, Timothy. "Yosemite Speed, Patagonia Summits." *American Alpine Journal* (2000): 66–74.

Pagel, Dave. "Great Innovations." *Climbing* magazine 192, (2000): 120–131.

Raleigh, Duane. "Get on the fast track." *Climbing* magazine 148 (November 1994): 146–151.

Raleigh, Duane, and Dave Anderson. "Tech Tip: Aid Climbing." *Climbing* magazine 189, (November 1999): 132.

Schneider, Steve. "Seize the Day." *Climbing* magazine no. 153 (June 1995): 90–99

Sharp, Alec. "Who's Your Friend?" *Mountain* 69 (September/October 1979.)

Thesenga, Jonathan. "The A Team." *Climbing* magazine, no. 192 (March 2000): 104–112.

Web sites

www.Speedclimb.com (Hans Florine's site about Yosemite Valley speed climbing records.)

www.wwwright.com/Climbing/coloradospeed.html (Bill Wright's site on Colorado speed climbing records.)

www.mountainzone.com

www.everest2000.com/base_camp/0523/babu_interview.html

www.rayjardine.com

www.royalrobbins.com

www.supertopo.com

www.touchstoneclimbing.com

www.ccrank.com

www.rocklist.com

www.birthdaychallenge.com